SELLING
YOUR
MARKETING
AGENCY

MAKING THE
MOST OF
YOUR MOST
IMPORTANT DEAL

DAVID RODNITZKY

WITH ROBERT GLAZER

This publication is designed to provide accurate and authoritative information in regard to the subject matter covered. It is sold with the understanding that neither the author nor the publisher is hereby engaged in offering or rendering legal, financial, or other professional services. If expert assistance is required, the services of a competent professional should be retained.

DEDICATION

To Rebecca, Zev, and Sammy. Thank you for supporting me through the ups and downs of selling 3Q (again and again and again)! M&A is all encompassing, and I couldn't have made it through long nights with lawyers and accountants without your unwavering support and patience.

TABLE OF CONTENTS

INTRODUCTION
The Accidental Empire Builder

In the last two decades, I've talked to hundreds of marketing agency founders of every kind. From founders who just started their agencies and are wondering why they quit their day job, to seasoned vets who've moved from the proverbial coffee shop to marble ensconced lobbies at the top of a swank New York high rise.

Most founders start their agency for one of three reasons:

- **I Can Do This Better!** Frustrated with the quality of service at their existing agency, they set out on their own, determined to deliver better results for clients.

- **I Can't Stand This Job Anymore!** Frustrated with internal politics, bureaucracy, limited promotion opportunities, or just a bad boss, these founders want to work for themselves because they can't stand the alternative.

- **Dumb Luck**. An unexpected pink slip or a move to a new city results in the founder being out of a job. While searching for a new opportunity, ex-clients call and ask if he's available for some contract work. After a few such calls, the founder-to-be realizes he can make it on his own and launches his agency.

Perhaps you noticed one reason conspicuously absent from this list: to build an agency and someday sell it for lots of money! Entrepreneurs who start tech companies know from day one that they're playing a game where winning is defined as an initial public offering (IPO) or acquisition. They raise money from venture capitalists who are playing the same game, and they hire employees who are lured into long hours in exchange for stock options that will pay off upon a company exit.

Agency founders don't do any of this. Instead, they just build their business and rejoice over small wins—scaling a client's business to new heights, opening an office in a new city, hiring another employee. Like any entrepreneur, the founder is excited by growth and doesn't mind the increasingly larger salary/profit share he gets every year. But selling? That isn't something that occupies much space in the mind of a growing agency's founder.

Then it happens. The founder starts to get calls from suitors. A large agency who lost a big client to the founder's agency or recently lost out on buying a competitor agency suddenly wants to know if he'd consider selling his business. An investment banker reaches out promising that she can get the founder millions of dollars if he lets her represent the business to potential acquirers. A **private equity**[1] investor pitches the founder on a **roll-up** strategy, where he'll combine the founder's business with other agencies to create an industry juggernaut.

---

[1]Terms in bold are defined in the glossary at the back of the book.

Unlike the tech founder—who has been planning for these conversations from day one, and has alignment from investors and employees to follow this path—the agency founder is completely unprepared for this. Should he even consider selling? Should he hire an investment banker? How much should the sales price be? How does he compare different offers? Should he get buy-in from the team? Will clients be OK with a sale?

And here's the rub: For most founders, this sales process is the one and only time they'll sell a business. Everyone else involved in the transaction—the buyer, lawyers, and investment bankers—likely has bought or sold dozens of agencies.

Founders who navigate these concerns properly might hit the jackpot—life-changing money, happy clients, happy team members, and peace of mind. Founders who do not may end up regretting passing on a sale as the biggest mistake of their life.

And here's the rub: For most founders, this sales process is the one and only time they'll sell a business. Everyone else involved in the transaction—the buyer, lawyers, and investment bankers—likely has bought or sold dozens of agencies. This puts the founder at a significant information disadvantage, forcing them to pay huge sums (often over $1 million) for experts to help guide him.

Ultimately, however, it's not always clear that the experts' incentives are fully aligned with that of the founder. Lawyers get paid by the hour, so they make money by dragging out the negotiations and bickering over irrelevant legal points. Investment bankers get paid when a deal closes, so they have an incentive to get the founder to sell quickly, even if the offer isn't perfect.

In other words, at the most important moment in a founder's business career, he has no choice but to rely on the advice of highly paid advisors who may steer him toward suboptimal outcomes.

This is not to say that investment banks and lawyers are malicious—most aren't! They're a valuable part of the team that a founder needs to build to get an enterprise-level sale done. That said, the more a founder can learn about agency **mergers and acquisitions (M&A)** prior to actually going through the sales process, the more likely it is that that founder will be able to distinguish between good and bad advice and make educated decisions that maximize the deal value.

That is the purpose of this book—to put you, the agency founder, on a level playing field, even if this is the first and only time you sell your agency, and to give you the benefit of hindsight from other founders who've already sold their businesses.

From deciding whether you even want to sell, to picking the right advisors, to negotiating a great deal, and integrating your agency post-sale, this book will help prepare you for every step of the agency sales process.

GETTING AN MBA IN M&A

I can teach all of this to you because I've been there. Since 2014, I've bought one agency and sold three (well, I actually sold the same agency three times).

My story begins in 2008. I had just quit my job as Vice President of Advertising at an ecommerce company in San Francisco. The timing couldn't have been worse—the world was about to enter into "The Great Recession," so jobs were drying up quickly. On top of that, my wife was expecting our first child, who was born almost exactly a month after my last day as a full-time employee.

In my first few months of being unemployed, I threw a bunch of ideas against the wall to see if any of them stuck. I started numerous affiliate websites hocking wrinkle cream, cash for gold, and insurance quotes online. I founded a conference dedicated to content marketing. I played online poker (and for a brief few days, I was actually doing quite well). And I fielded a lot of calls from my friends in the marketing world who wanted help with their companies' online marketing campaigns.

Over that first year, my affiliate sites went belly-up (specifically, they were hacked, and I couldn't fix them back to profitability), the conference I founded had two semi-successful shows but never caught on, and I went from up $3000 in poker to down $1000 in about a month. The only thing that was consistently doing well was my consulting business.

In my first year of consulting, I made about 75% of the full-time salary at my last job. Oh, and I had to pay for my own benefits. So financially, it didn't seem like a great decision. But I was having a blast. Rather than a 45-minute commute twice a day, I had a three-minute commute to the local coffee shop. Instead of dealing with corporate politics, I was my own boss. And it felt really great to be an entrepreneur.

That was pretty much the extent of my business strategy: keep making enough money to pay the bills and not have to go back to a real job!

Over the next couple of years, that strategy changed. I was getting a lot of inbound referrals requesting my services, and I couldn't handle all the business. I had to make a choice: Remain a solo consultant and turn away a lot of business, or try to turn my consultancy into an agency. I decided to try the agency route. I hired my first employee and found that I could still deliver great results to clients, even if I wasn't the only one doing the work. That first employee soon became a few employees. My initial focus on search engine marketing (buying ads on Google) soon expanded into additional channels, such as Facebook advertising, search engine optimization (SEO), and landing page optimization.

I eventually opened an office. Initially, I got a WeWork-like office that I could use two days a week. Then I got my own 600 square foot office (it fit, at most, five people). Once that office was too cramped, I upgraded to a 1500 square foot office. Then we opened an office in Chicago. Then San Diego. Then New York.

Fast forward to 2014. My consulting gig was now an agency with more than 100 people in five offices across the US. That year, I was having a casual coffee with a friend of mine from another agency who asked me if I'd consider acquiring his business. A few months later we acquired iSearchMedia and added another 50 team members to 3Q Digital.

In 2014, the business did $14 million of revenue with a 35% annual growth rate. We started to win big, brand-name clients. Google told us we were one of their top independent agencies (collectively, our clients were spending around $500 million a year with Google).

I started getting a lot of calls from potential acquirers. Knowing nothing about the mergers and acquisitions (M&A) space for agencies, I brought in experts, hiring an investment banker to guide me through the process (which, as we'll discuss, is a highly choreographed and nuanced dance!).

In late 2014, the investment banker solicited bids from interested parties. After a lot of back and forth, we chose to sell the company in early 2015 to Harte Hanks, a publicly traded marketing services business out of Texas. The deal paid us $30 million up front and promised a potential earnout (more on that term later) of an additional $35 million in three years if we hit our growth goals.

The deal was a dream come true for me and my team. Obviously, the financial outcome was well beyond anything I ever thought I'd achieve. But I was equally excited about partnering with Harte Hanks and building an industry leader in the online marketing space.

Alas, things didn't turn out the way I expected. In 2017, Harte Hanks decided to sell 3Q Digital. By this point, we were on track to do more than $35 million in annual revenue. After negotiations with numerous potential buyers, in 2018, Harte Hanks sold 3Q Digital back to me and my co-founders (the founders of iSearchMedia, the company we acquired) for $10 million in cash and the cancellation of the $35 million of earnout payments that we were owed.

3Q was independent again, and it felt great! Over the next year, we continued to grow rapidly. We were now close to 300 team members and had 10 offices, including one in Europe and one in Asia.

Once again, our rapid growth attracted the interest of potential acquirers. As with 2014, we hired an investment banker and negotiated with two private equity companies out of Chicago, PSP Partners and Erie Street Growth Partners. In early 2019, we announced a sale of the majority of the company to PSP and Erie Street, we hired our first CFO, moved our headquarters to Chicago, brought in a professional CEO (which enabled me to take a much needed step back from running the business and focus on strategy), survived and even flourished during the pandemic, and scaled the business to over 500 employees. Our spend with Google was now over $2 billion a year.

In May of 2022, we announced that 3Q had joined forces with DEPT, a large Holland-based agency. Collectively, the two companies now have more than 3000 employees.

So, yeah, in the eight years between 2014 and 2022, I was involved in four M&A deals.

If you're like me, you understand that "learning on someone else's dime" is a great benefit to your business. I've spent a lot of dimes on M&A—tens of millions of dimes in fact! I'm writing this book because I love helping agency founders avoid some of the mistakes I made. It often feels like the deck is stacked against the founder. In many cases, the people you are negotiating against (like a large agency or a professional investor) have years of experience focused on buying and selling companies. I hope that by sharing my experiences, you'll be able to level the playing field in your negotiations.

HOW TO USE THIS BOOK

Depending on how close you are to potentially selling your agency, you don't need to read every chapter of this book. Ultimately, there are four broad topics covered.

First, we'll talk about *whether it makes sense to sell your agency.* This includes the first three chapters of the book: Are you mentally ready to sell? How much is your agency worth? Will the sale meet your financial needs?

These chapters are important for any agency founder who is in the early stages of thinking about a potential sale but has not yet fully committed to an exit. Read these chapters to help you decide whether to move forward with a sale or not.

Next, in chapters four through six, we *review the mechanics of putting your agency up for sale.* Who buys agencies (and what are the advantages and disadvantages of different buyers)? When do you need an investment bank, and how do you choose one? How do you find the right potential buyers and get them to bid on your agency?

These chapters are relevant to founders who've already decided to consider a sale and are now on the precipice of hiring experts and contacting potential buyers.

The third section is devoted to the *sale itself.* This includes chapters seven through nine. How do you find and choose a great law firm? How do you prepare for due diligence? How do you negotiate fairly but aggressively? What are the most important legal terms to negotiate? How and when do you notify team members and clients? If you've selected a buyer and are ready to negotiate your contract, read these sections.

Lastly, the final chapters in the book talk about *post-sale life for founders.* Should you continue to be CEO? How do you deal with seller's remorse? If you want to leave your firm, how do you leave gracefully? Even if you sold your agency years ago, this section may still be helpful to you.

One other important point: Most of my experience selling agencies has been between two enterprise-level companies, e.g., both the buyer and the seller are businesses that have scaled to millions of dollars of profit with the enterprise value of the seller exceeding $20 million. While there are definitely similarities between a deal valued at $5 million and a deal valued at $500 million, the mechanics of these two deals will be vastly different.

This is particularly true with respect to the number of outside experts who will be involved (lawyers, investment bankers, accountants, M&A consultants, and so on) and the complexity of the legal documents.

If the value of your deal does not reach enterprise-level prices, you may not need to talk to dozens of potential suitors. You might not need an army of high-priced lawyers and experts to close the deal.

And you will also likely have a lot less leverage to get all the contractual terms you want included in the final purchase agreement.

Thus, as you read the section on selling your agency and negotiating your deal, keep in mind that these sections were written from the perspective of a seller of an enterprise-level agency. If your agency isn't quite at that level, you will need to recalibrate your needs and expectations.

FIRST THINGS FIRST
To Sell or Not to Sell

A few years ago, I had a phone conversation with a fellow agency founder. He told me that his business was exploding—he expected 50% year-over-year growth (Note: this wasn't a one-person shop—it was already a big company).

He got me pretty excited about his business, so much so that I asked him if he'd consider an acquisition offer. His response: "David, why would I sell now when I'm about to have the best year in the history of the business?"

My first reaction was that his comment reminded me of this exchange from *Star Wars*.

> Underling: We've analyzed their attack, sir, and there's a danger. Should I have your ship standing by?
>
> Grand Moff Tarkin: Evacuate? In our moment of triumph?
>
> (Shortly thereafter, the Death Star is blown into a million pieces).[1]

---

[1] *Star Wars*, George, Lucas, director, Twentieth Century Fox, 1977.

As I'll explain, that reaction is much more indicative of how I think about when to sell a business. In no way does it reflect on the likelihood of long-term success for my friend. My personality is such that I always want to de-risk myself by "taking chips off the table." So if someone made me an acquisition offer and I knew that my next year was going to be fantastic, my instinct would be to immediately consider the acquisition, because I would be bargaining from a position of strength and could command a good value while simultaneously de-risking.

In truth, neither my response nor my friend's response is inherently correct. Indeed, the answer will and should be different for every entrepreneur.

THIS CHAPTER IS ABOUT EMOTION, NOT MONEY

The experience I'm sharing in this chapter is not intended to help you predict whether a sale of your business will make you more money than keeping the business and running it.

This chapter isn't about knowing how to maximize profit. We'll talk about that later.

Instead, this is about the emotional decision to sell. Selling your business, as the cliché goes, is like selling your baby. I've talked to founders who've had very successful sales, and shortly thereafter have seen their previously happy marriage end in divorce—in large part, because the founders didn't realize how much *not* being an entrepreneur would change the dynamics of their relationship. My friend who didn't want to sell noted that "postpartum depression" is a real issue among entrepreneurs who sell their companies.

By the same token, I know founders who've turned down a big acquisition offer and then seen their company decline precipitously in value, sometimes to zero. For these founders, the constant question of "what if" and the pain of missed opportunity haunt them to this day.

With that in mind, I've come up with four questions to ask yourself to assess the emotional consequences of selling your business.

? QUESTION #1
How Important Is Control to You?

I started my business because I was frustrated with what I saw as bad management, bad culture, and bad decision making at the companies at which I'd worked. As an example, prior to starting my agency, I worked at a company that received an "F" from the Better Business Bureau for seriously bad customer service. At another company, I was told by the CEO that my annual bonus would be reduced if I used too much printer toner!

I got fed up with not having the control to prevent bad decisions and started a small consulting firm in 2008. From day one (when it was just me), to the present, I developed very specific core values and core beliefs that dictate how I expect everyone in the company to act, and what they can expect from me and my executives.

When you sell your business, you lose some control over decision making. No matter what the buyer promises you—and even to some degree, what you negotiate in your sales contract—selling your business means that someone other than you is going to have a significant say in how decisions are made, or will have the final decision-making authority. Everything from who is on your team, to the company culture, where your offices are located, and what types of clients you take on—you trade some of this control away once you accept payment from a buyer!

For some entrepreneurs, this isn't a big deal. If, for example, the business is a means to an end (making a lot of money through a sale is your core objective, or you're burnt out), having someone else come in and wrest control isn't a big deal. For others, either because they love power, have very strong opinions about how to run the business, or are just hard-wired to be control freaks, selling can be emotionally disastrous.

? QUESTION #2
Are You Tired or Just Getting Started?

When I started my company, I was driven to prove to myself and to others that I could build a great business. I worked like crazy to build, build, and build. And the truth is, even today, after building 3Q from one person in a coffee shop to hundreds of people, I've still got a chip on my shoulder, albeit it's a different one. My internal mission statement at 3Q has been that *we're saving clients from inept agencies*—I'm driven to grab market share from bloated multinational agencies.

Most entrepreneurs, while perhaps not sharing my exact psychological reasons, have a fire that drives them to start and grow their business. The greatest entrepreneurs in the world—Steve Jobs, Elon Musk, Richard Branson—have a passion that never leaves them, no matter how many billions of dollars or successful businesses they've created.

But that may not be true for you. At some point, you may wake up and realize that the fun you had building your business has diminished. Maybe it feels like it's just become a job, or that other people get to do the fun stuff and you're left with the hard decisions and tough conversations.

My entrepreneur friend gave me one more interesting perspective on this question (which he admits that he did not invent): Create a 2x2 matrix with two questions. First, do you enjoy what you do? Second, do you know what you want to do next? If you enjoy your job and don't know what you want to do next, you should keep going. If you hate it and know what else you want to do, sell. The other two are in between.

Do you know what you want to do next?

An important point: The degree to which you've made yourself irrelevant to the future success of the business significantly impacts whether an acquirer will buy your business and then let you move on. In a way, the job of an entrepreneur is to "fire yourself" from as many jobs as possible. When I started the business, I was Head of Finance, Head of Sales, Head of Client Services, and Chief Costco Orderer. The more I was able to hire talented people to take on these roles, the more I built "enterprise value" in the company, which is another way of saying that I could get hit by a truck and the business would continue without me, irrespective of whether or not I was the owner. If you've built a business that has enterprise value and you're tired of running the business, a sale where you exit the business is a very real possibility.

? QUESTION #3
How Important Is Growing Your Business?

I have a lot of friends that have built "lifestyle businesses." They have few or no employees, no office, and take on enough work to make a good living but almost never put in a 40-hour work week. I frequently see them posting photos on Facebook of their numerous exotic vacations. This sort of business isn't acquirable, but it can create excellent work-life balance and a very comfortable lifestyle.

That's never been my style. Indeed, because I was so scarred by the bad experiences I had working for other people, I was paranoid about building a business that could have a few rough patches and still survive. I wanted to make sure that I would never have to close the business and work for someone else. Coupled with my previously mentioned desire to prove myself and take work away from competitors, growth is hugely important to me.

Acquirers buy businesses not only for the value of the business today, but because they believe they can grow the acquired business. Sometimes that growth comes from synergies with the acquiring business, hiring professional management, merging with or acquiring other businesses, or by infusing cash into the business to make important investments that lead to growth.

Put another way, selling your business to the right buyer with the right strategy should accelerate your growth. If growth is important to you—either because you need it for your psyche or because you need more growth just to survive—an acquisition may be the perfect decision. On the other hand, if you like long vacations and a 20-hour work week, or just don't value growth that much, the opportunity for growth shouldn't drive your decision.

How Much Risk Do You Like to Take?

If I sit down at the blackjack table with $200 and turn that $200 into $500, I immediately take $300 and put it in my pocket and then keep playing with the "house money," thereby guaranteeing a profit. Other people go from $200 to $500 and then try to turn that $500 into $1500, knowing that they may end up losing all of it.

This is the essence of my conversation with my friend who couldn't fathom selling his company on the cusp of a banner year. From my conservative perspective, taking money off the table while the company is doing great is a smart, de-risking decision; from his, the future potential of the company emboldens him to keep the business independent and go for a much bigger outcome.

First, the difference between $1 million dollars and $2 million dollars is a lot less than the difference between zero and $1 million dollars. Second, it's better to sell your company too early than too late.

In fact, shortly after this conversation happened, the COVID pandemic disrupted the world economy, and my friend suddenly saw his agency's bookings drop dramatically. He realized that much of his net worth was tied up in his agency and that a "Black Swan" event like COVID or just bad luck could destroy his nest egg overnight. Fortunately, the business ended up thriving after a few down months, and my friend was able to sell for a great valuation, but COVID taught him a valuable lesson about risk and financial diversification.

I have two adages that I share with entrepreneurs that describe my mindset. First, the difference between $1 million dollars and $2 million dollars is a lot less than the difference between zero and $1 million dollars. Second, it's better to sell your company too early than too late.

I worked at a company that was run by a 20-something entrepreneur. He had an offer to sell the company for $500 million and rejected it. A few years later, the company was sold for just enough money to pay off debts. By contrast, Mark Zuckerberg was offered $900 million for Facebook, turned down that offer, and now runs a company worth hundreds of billions of dollars.

My litmus test here is simple: if you turn down an offer of life-changing money and your business declines, how much will that decision haunt you? For some founders, the money is irrelevant. These founders get so much joy out of just running their business that missing out on a big exit is irrelevant.

For other founders, accepting an offer and then seeing their company increase in value many times over is devastating, so they'd rather risk saying no to a good offer, even if it means missing out on a better one.

Again, there's no one answer. You have to figure out how much risk you want to take and whether you care more about de-risking or maximizing upside.

ROSEBUD

The classic film *Citizen Kane* is about an entrepreneur who relentlessly grows a massive business empire (an homage to William Randolph Hearst). Kane seemingly has everything—the decadent mansion, the ear of the powerful, the respect of his peers—and yet, on his deathbed, he utters a simple word: Rosebud. We find out at the end of the movie that Rosebud was the name of his childhood sled and that the one thing he wanted in life but never had was the love of his parents. The point is obvious: all the money, all the power, and all the success in the world is secondary to the ultimate goal: happiness.

Selling your business can be one of the best moments in your life, or it can be the most regrettable decision you'll ever make. If you make your decision to sell or not to sell by trying to optimize your happiness—rather than only optimizing for financial gain—you'll likely end up making the right choice.

ALTERNATIVES TO SELLING YOUR AGENCY

Maybe you've decided that you aren't ready to sell yet. And at the same time, you also don't want to maintain the status quo. What can you do? As an agency founder, you have a few alternatives to an outright sale of your agency.

☑ OPTION #1: Become Non-Operational

If you don't want to continue to run the agency day-to-day, hiring or promoting a team member to CEO to replace you is a viable solution. This strategy enables you to be still involved in the business, maintain all or most of your equity, but also reduce the time commitment and stress-level associated with the business.

In some cases, a founder renounces all of her daily responsibilities, moving to a board-level position that has oversight but no day-to-day participation in the business. In others, the founder takes a lesser role than the CEO (like COO, President, or Head of Strategy), and still stays involved in the day-to-day business, just not as the CEO.

This strategy can be a double-win for you. Find the right CEO, and the business may grow faster than it did under your guidance, enabling you to reduce your time in the business and simultaneously increase the value of your equity.

Of course, if you enjoy/need to be in control of the business, this option may not be viable. And there's always the chance that the new CEO isn't a fit and doesn't move the company in the right direction.

✅ OPTION #2: Raise Debt Financing

One of the benefits of selling your agency is that you get the backing of a larger organization that can invest more resources in your agency, helping you grow faster than you would as a stand-alone business. An alternative growth strategy that keeps the founder in control of the business is to raise debt financing. Debt financing means taking a loan and using the loan to invest in business growth. If you have strong financials, a lender may be willing to loan you a multiple of your annual profit. For example, if you achieved $5 million of profit in the last 12 months, a bank may be willing to loan you $15 million (3X your profit).

For particularly strong agencies, you may be able to exchange some of your equity for debt and take the cash for yourself. This is known as a **recapitalization**, or recap for short. In this scenario, you might raise $15 million from a bank and take $10 million for yourself, leaving $5 million for the company to use to grow. This enables you to de-risk yourself without giving up control of the business.

For large agencies, you can often raise debt financing with no personal guarantee, meaning that if the company fails and owes money to a bank, you aren't personally liable to pay the debt (and you can avoid personal bankruptcy). For most agencies (under several million dollars of annual **earnings before interest, tax, deduction, and amortization or EBITDA**), however, banks will require a personal guarantee on debt, meaning that if you're too aggressive with your financing, you might risk personal liability if the company defaults on the loan.

As we'll discuss later, this is a standard tactic used by private equity firms after they acquire an agency. When it works, debt financing (also known as leverage), enables a business to grow and increase its valuation without giving up any equity. The downside is that, when it doesn't work, the debt payments can bankrupt the company!

✓ OPTION #3: Become an Employee-Owned Business

If you want to de-risk yourself but can't imagine someone outside of your culture owning the business, selling the company to your employees is a good option. In this scenario, the founder decides to sell all or many of his shares to employees over a period of years. This is different from an **employee stock option program (ESOP)**, where a company gives options to employees. In that case, when options are purchased by the company, the company retains the proceeds. When transferring to employee-ownership, every time an employee buys a share of the company, the money is paid to the founders.

Selling shares to employees comes with risks. For starters, once employees' shares vest, they're usually free to leave the company and retain their equity. Given the high turnover that agencies experience, that can mean having a meaningful percentage of the company's stock owned by people who no longer work at the agency. It may even be the case that some of the owners of your company stock are now working for a competitor!

Stock plans also require lawyers, both during the formation of the plan and for ongoing maintenance. In the early days of 3Q Digital, I created a stock plan and awarded shares to top employees. Unfortunately, I wasn't aware of a federal tax statute known as 409(a), which requires companies to set stock option values based on a series of IRS rules. When a lawyer subsequently reviewed the company stock plan, he noted that it was not in compliance with 409(a). As a result, we had to spend tens of thousands of dollars to fix the plan.

☑ OPTION #4: Sell a Minority Stake

If you want to take some cash out of the business but you still want control, you can sell a minority stake of the business to outside investors. While most investors only want to buy agencies in which they have majority ownership, there are rare instances where investors will buy a minority stake in an agency. Typically, this happens with large, highly successful agencies with significant EBITDA (say, $50 million or more a year). These agencies are on a clear path to going public or selling in the near future, and investors may be so excited about the company that they'll take a minority stake.

- Selling is not the right choice for every agency founder. Many founders will either never be ready or aren't currently ready to sell.

- Factors to consider include how willing you are to give up control of your business, whether you still have the energy to continue leading your agency, how important it is to grow your business, and how much risk you're willing to take (e.g., saying no to a large sum of money and taking a risk that you can make more money staying independent).

- There are also alternatives to selling that can give founders flexibility or liquidity while still maintaining a large amount of control. This includes bringing in a professional CEO to replace you, raising debt financing instead of equity financing, selling some of your shares to your employees, and accepting a minority investment from an investor.

- Ultimately, every founder has different needs and is at different stages of their life and professional career. There's no simple answer that works for everyone. Selling or not selling your agency is the most important business decision in most founders' lives. As such, founders should think long and hard about their options and resist the urge to make quick decisions.

CHAPTER TWO

OK, NOW LET'S TALK ABOUT MONEY

After reading the previous chapter, you may have decided that you're not ready to sell your agency, regardless of the price an acquirer might pay for it. If so, great! Put this book back on the shelf and keep running your business. You can always reconsider your options at a future point! Assuming, however, that you're at least open to the idea of an acquisition, read on.

This chapter is not about how much your agency is worth—that will be discussed in a later chapter. Instead, the topic here is figuring out your financial goals and how these align with a potential sale of your agency.

WHAT'S YOUR NUMBER?

Kurt Vonnegut wrote the following obituary of author Joseph Heller in *The New Yorker*:

> *True story, Word of Honor:*
>
> *Joseph Heller, an important and funny writer*
>
> *now dead,*
>
> *and I were at a party given by a billionaire*
>
> *on Shelter Island.*
>
> *I said, "Joe, how does it make you feel*
>
> *to know that our host only yesterday*
>
> *may have made more money*
>
> *than your novel 'Catch-22'*
>
> *has earned in its entire history?"*
>
> *And Joe said, "I've got something he can never have."*
>
> *And I said, "What on earth could that be, Joe?"*
>
> *And Joe said, "The knowledge that I've got enough."*
>
> *Not bad! Rest in peace!"*[1]

The first step in this process is to figure out "your number"—the amount of money that will make you happy in life.

Figuring out your number is a topic that could take up an entire book. For most people, the number is a combination of a few factors:

- Having enough money to make it through retirement without worry. For some, it means being able to retire right away, even if they're years away from the normal retirement age.

- Being able to buy a dream item (like a second house or a fancy car).

---

[1] *The New Yorker*, May 16, 2005.

- Setting up a trust for your children.

- Donating to a charity.

Of course, the number is dependent on your lifestyle, where you live, and how old you are. A 75-year-old who lives frugally in a low-cost area of the world might need $1.5 million to live her dream retirement. By contrast, a 30-year-old in Silicon Valley might need $10 million or more.

I don't have a magic formula that answers this question for every reader. Talking to a trusted financial advisor who understands the nuances of your goal and financial needs is a great step to figure this out.

But having a rough idea of your financial goal is important because it helps you understand whether an offer to buy your business is going to get you where you want to go.

Keep in mind that many agency founders are legally prevented from working in the agency space for many years after they sell their business—it's common to include a **non-compete** clause in the agency acquisition agreement that the founder must sign. If all you know how to do is run an agency, this makes you unemployable for many years with no annual income stream.

Let's assume that your number is $4 million and that you get an offer for $4 million—your number!—to sell the business, but you must also sign a four-year non-compete. After taxes (assuming 30% state and federal, which will vary dramatically by state), you get $2.8 million. If you can make 4% after taxes per year on these proceeds (most financial advisors recommend choosing a conservative rate of return when calculating how much money you need for a specific goal), your annual investment income is $112,000. Since you probably need more than that to maintain your standard of living, you'll have to dip into your nest egg every year. That might be fine for you, or you might suddenly realize that you need more savings to get you where you want to go.

Or, you might have a skill set that enables you to earn income every year, perhaps as a consultant, or by starting another agency if your contract allows it. In that case, the equation changes dramatically. If you can make $150,000 a year in income ($105,000 after taxes), suddenly you're making $217,000 annually. This might be enough to live your life without touching your nest egg.

Lastly, keep in mind that establishing your number and reaching your number are two different things. You can declare that $20 million is your number, but if your business is worth no more than $5 million, you have to decide whether it's worth selling even if you can't hit your number. Some businesses that are worth $5 million today will be worth $20 million in a few years, but others (and in the agency world, that's likely most of them) will never become that valuable. Buyers don't care whether you hit your number or not, they'll offer you what they think your agency is worth—period!

HEDONIC ADAPTATION

There's a concept called **hedonic adaptation** (also known as the hedonic treadmill) that is relevant here. Hedonic adaptation refers to the tendency for people to adapt quickly to changes in their level of happiness or well-being. This means that over time, people tend to return to their baseline level of happiness even after experiencing positive or negative events, such as getting a promotion, winning the lottery, or going through a divorce.

Imagine, for example, buying a new BMW. When you were a kid, this was your dream car. You never thought you'd ever be able to afford one. Now here you are, driving down the street in a $75,000 German luxury car. The high of owning this amazing car, however, only lasts for a few months. Pretty soon, you just get used to driving a BMW. You start to think, "This Beemer is nice, but my neighbor has a Mercedes. It sure would be nice to have one of those." This is hedonic adaptation.

Hedonic adaptation impacts agency owners. Perhaps when you started your agency, you dreamed of selling for $5 million. With that amount of money, you reasoned, you could have a great retirement and take a few amazing trips every year. Fast forward five years. Suddenly you have a business that's worth $5 million. You can sell today and hit your number! But then you start thinking, "Hmm, $5 million is great, but I've always dreamed of owning a house in Maui. Maybe I need $8 million."

A few years later, the business is worth $8 million, and a buyer is ready to pay you for it. You think: "$8 million is amazing but . . . I've always thought it would be fun to own a winery. And having a boat sure would be nice. Maybe I need $15 million."

When you fall into this trap, no amount of money is ever enough. Sometimes, this results in disaster. Not all agencies increase in value year after year. I know several agency owners who rejected a great offer, only to see the business struggle and decline. In a few cases, the businesses have gone bankrupt, and the owner walked away with nothing.

I'm not suggesting that you can only choose your number once and never modify it. But I do think it's important to step back, determine what's really important to you, and not get caught on the hedonic treadmill—never happy with where you are financially.

It also may be the case that your number is way higher than any offer you could reasonably expect to receive for your agency. In that case, you may still want to sell. Perhaps the money you get from an offer today will eventually enable you to get to your number after a few years of smart investing. You may be ready to move onto a new phase of your life. Or you may be convinced that this is the best offer you could ever get for your business.

Remember, the decision to sell is complicated, and it's rarely the case that you get exactly what you want. Having a number in mind helps you act more level-headed when someone throws a lot of money at you, but it's also not the end-all, be-all.

THE IMPORTANCE OF TIME

If you're a baseball fan, you may have heard the story of Bobby Bonilla's contract with the New York Mets. In 2000, the Mets owed Bonilla $5.9 million. But rather than paying Bonilla in one lump sum, they negotiated a deferred payment. The Mets gave Bonilla 8% interest annually (and compounding) until 2011, and then agreed to make equal payments on the total amount for 25 years (until 2035).

That 8% compounding interest turned into a $29.8 million liability, meaning that until 2035, the Mets are required to pay $1.19 million a year to a player who hasn't been with the team since 2001!

As the above story shows, the timing of when you get paid can have massive financial consequences. But timing is not just about how much money you can make. For example, if I asked you whether you would rather have $1 million today or $10 million in three years, from a financial perspective, the answer is easy: wait for the $10 million. But what if you have a daughter who's going away to college in two years, and you really want to have as much time to spend with her as possible? That time to you is priceless, so not maximizing your financial outcome is OK if it enables you to focus your time on your daughter.

These considerations are highly relevant when contemplating a sale of your agency. Let's start by talking about the math underlying an agency sale.

One of the benefits of selling your agency is that you're paid in advance for the future success of your business. If you get a 5X multiple on your last 12 months of profit, you're getting paid for five years of current earnings.

And don't forget to consider the time-value of money. A dollar today is worth more than $1.50 in 10 years, simply because you can invest that dollar and make a return on it. So it goes with agency sales. If you sell today and get paid in advance for future profit, you can invest that money. If you don't sell, your money isn't working for you.

Imagine you own an agency that makes $1 million of profit (EBITDA) a year (and, for the sake of argument, let's say that you withdraw all of that as distributions at the end of each year). Assume also that your profit is growing at 20% a year. An acquirer is willing to offer you $5 million in cash to buy your business. If you accept this offer, you'd get $3.5 million immediately (assuming 30% combined federal and state taxes on the $5 million purchase), plus you'd get another $594,000 in interest income over the next five years (assuming a 4% after-tax rate of return) for a total of $4.09 million (See Table 2-1).

If you kept the business and it continued to grow at 20% a year, at the end of five years, you'd have $5.6 million in cash distributions and investment interest (again, after state and federal taxes and assuming after-tax returns of 4% a year on your investments). If you decided to sell at the end of this five year period, your annual EBITDA would now be $2.07 million. Assuming an acquirer would pay you 5X your EBITDA, you would get a $10.3 million purchase price for your business. The combination of five years of distributions, interest income, and $7.2 million in after-taxes proceeds from the acquisition would result in a total return of $12.8 million. (See Table 2-2).

Of course, this assumes you continue to grow the business. What happens if you don't? What happens if—instead of growing 20% a year—your profit declines by 20% a year? In that scenario, at the end of five years, you've collected a total of $2.6 million in distributions. And since your business is in decline, you're unlikely to have many interested acquirers. If someone did buy it, they would likely offer you a lower EBITDA multiple. Assuming a 3X multiple on your Year Five EBITDA of $409,600, your total return over five years after taxes would be $3.4 million. (See Table 2-3.)

This is all a little hard to explain via text. These tables may help you visually see the difference in these scenarios.

TABLE 2-1: Sell Your Business for 5X Multiple in Year One on $1 Million EBITDA							TOTAL
	YEAR 1	YEAR 2	YEAR 3	YEAR 4	YEAR 5	END OF YEAR 5 VALUE	
EBITDA (20% Expected Annual Growth)	$ -	$ -	$ -	$ -	$ -		$ -
Annual Proceeds After Taxes from EBITDA (State and Federal - 30%)							
Cumulative Proceeds from Annual Distributions		$ -	$ -	$ -	$ -		
Acquisition at 5X	$ 5,000,000	$ -	$ -	$ -	$ -	$ -	
Proceeds After Taxes from Acquisition (State and Federal - 30%)	$ 3,500,000						$ 3,500,000
4% Annual Interest from Your Investments (After Taxes)		$ 140,000	$ 145,600	$ 151,424	$ 157,481		$ 594,505
TOTAL							$ 4,094,505

TABLE 2-2: Keep Business for Five Years, 20% Annual EBITDA Growth, Sell for 5X Multiple in Year Six

	YEAR 1	YEAR 2	YEAR 3	YEAR 4	YEAR 5	END OF YEAR 5 VALUE	TOTAL
EBITDA (20% Expected Annual Growth)	$ 1,000,000	$ 1,200,000	$ 1,440,000	$ 1,728,000	$ 2,073,600		
Annual Proceeds After Taxes (State and Federal - 30%)	$ 700,000	$ 840,000	$ 1,008,000	$ 1,209,600	$ 1,451,520		
Cumulative Proceeds from Annual Distributions		$ 1,540,000	$ 2,548,000	$ 3,757,600	$ 5,209,120		$ 5,209,120
Acquisition at 5X	$ -	$ -	$ -	$ -	$ -	$ 10,368,000	
Proceeds After Taxes from Acquisition (State and Federal - 30%)						$ 7,257,600	$ 7,257,600
4% Annual Interest from Your Investments (After Taxes)		$ 28,000	$ 61,600	$ 101,920	$ 150,304		$ 341,824
TOTAL							$ 12,808,544

TABLE 2-3: Keep Business for Five Years, 20% Annual EBITDA Decline, Sell for 3X Multiple in Year Six

	YEAR 1	YEAR 2	YEAR 3	YEAR 4	Year 5	END OF YEAR 5 VALUE	TOTAL
EBITDA (20% Annual Decline)	$ 1,000,000	$ 800,000	$ 640,000	$ 512,000	$ 409,600		$ 2,353,120
Annual Proceeds After Taxes (State and Federal - 30%)	$ 700,000	$ 560,000	$ 448,000	$ 358,400	$ 286,720		
Cumulative Proceeds from Annual Distributions		$ 1,260,000	$ 1,708,000	$ 2,066,400	$ 2,353,120		
Acquisition at 3X	$ -	$ -	$ -	$ -	$ -	$ 1,228,800	
Proceeds After Taxes from Acquisition (State and Federal - 30%)						$ 860,160	$ 860,160
4% Annual Interest from Your Investments (After Taxes)		$ 28,000	$ 50,400	$ 68,320	$ 82,656		$ 229,376
TOTAL							$ 3,442,656

So, just in this one scenario, you have returns ranging from $3.4 million to $12.8 million over a five-year period. Time is relevant not only because of the time-value of money but also because of the amount of time commitment you must put into the business. Again, if you have a daughter leaving for college in a couple of years, you may decide that reducing or eliminating your time in the business immediately is worth eschewing future gains.

UNDERSTANDING RISK

Risk is crucially important to your decision. When your agency is doing well, it's easy to assume that your growth will continue year-after-year. Selling while your agency is performing well feels like you're leaving a lot of money on the table. But selling guarantees you a lump sum payout. One of the adages I live by is it's better to sell too early than too late.

None of us can really predict the future. It's entirely possible that—rather than selling too early and watching your agency's value sky-rocket in the years following your sale—you may be selling at the height of your agency's value. You might lose your biggest client and see your financial performance plummet. Your industry might be revolutionized by new technology rendering your core value proposition obsolete (AI anyone?). The economy may crash, and numerous clients may terminate their contracts. New regulations may destroy your business. Your top employees may leave. Competitors may unleash a solution superior to yours. Likely acquirers may buy other companies and no longer need your agency. A family emergency may require you to spend less time in the business, reducing the company's performance.

Indeed, over the last decade—and in particular between 2020 and 2022—agency valuations have been at all-time highs. Agencies that might have sold for 8X EBITDA in 2010 sold for as much as 20X in 2020. Historically low interest rates and a booming economy allowed buyers to borrow a lot of money and make aggressive, sometimes ridiculous bids for agencies. By late 2022, however, the tide had turned. Interest rates rose, stock prices and valuations dropped, and the seller's market disappeared. Agencies who decided not to sell in 2021, on the assumption that valuations would continue to climb higher and higher, might have missed a golden opportunity to cash out at the top.

The dance between buyer and seller is one that considers risk and return on both sides, but ultimately is an imprecise process.

Anyone who has run a business for more than a few months knows that there are always ups and downs, and many of these are unpredictable. With a crystal ball, deciding to sell or hold would be incredibly easy. Alas—to my knowledge—no such device yet exists (please tell me if you discover one). At the end of the day, acquirers make offers based on a combination of a company's current performance and the anticipated future performance. They, too, have to hedge their bets about the future and thus can never offer you the full value of your future earnings. So the dance between buyer and seller is one that considers risk and return on both sides, but ultimately is an imprecise process.

PUTTING IT ALL TOGETHER

The amount of money you need, when you need/want it, and how much risk you're willing to take is a highly personal calculus. That said, it's a calculus you should think about before beginning to talk to acquirers. Once you've thought through the type of offer you're willing to take, you enter into negotiations with a point-of-view, rather than just reacting to whatever is put in front of you. You may not get everything you want, and you may make the wrong decision (in terms of maximizing the value of a deal), but you'll at least feel like you made a well-reasoned decision.

KEY TAKEAWAYS FROM THIS CHAPTER

- Founders should know the answer to three key questions before they embark on a potential sales process:
  - How much money do I really need?
  - When do I need or want this money?
  - How much risk I am willing to take with my money?

- It's easy to fall into the hedonic adaptation trap, where no amount of money is ever enough. Founders who always reset their "number" once they hit it will find themselves on a treadmill, never able to stop striving for more money.

- Accepting a big payment today may be the right decision, especially if that money allows you to focus on important life goals (like spending time with your family, starting a nonprofit, or even launching a new business). At the same time, delaying payment may be the right decision for a founder who sees a lot of future upside in his business and who doesn't really need a lot of money in the near term.

- Every decision involves risk. Different people have different appetites for risk. Taking a lot of money upfront reduces risk but also reduces the total potential upside for the founder. Taking little money upfront creates the potential for a big future payment but increases the risk that the founder gets little to nothing if the agency performance declines.

CHAPTER THREE

HOW MUCH IS MY AGENCY WORTH?

At a press conference in the 1960s, Bob Dylan was asked by a journalist, "How many protest singers are there like you?" Without missing a beat and in a perfect monotone, Dylan answered: "136."[1]

Dylan recognized the absurdity of the question: You can't quantify the number of protest singers in the world, the way you might calculate the average cost of gasoline or the fastest time in the 100-meter dash.

Quantifying the value of an agency is not quite as obtuse as the question posed to Dylan, but it's also far less concrete than knowing the cost of a gallon of gas. There are many factors that figure into the value of an agency, and some of these factors can't be measured. As a result, whatever valuation someone determines, the number will always be caveated with a lot of asterisks and expressions like, "It depends."

---

[1] Bob Dylan, Protest Songs You've Probably Never Heard, September 18, 1965, Gaslight Records, (https://gaslightrecords.com/articles/10-bob-dylan-protest-songs-youve-probably-never-heard#).

Before diving into the factors that determine an agency's worth, it's important to add two caveats. First, beware the Lake Wobegon effect. This is a reference to the old NPR show *Prairie Home Companion*, which takes place in the fictional town of Lake Wobegon, "where all the children are above average."[2]

If you go into a sales process with the expectation that you will get offers significantly higher than the mean, you may be disappointed and you may end up turning down a very good offer.

The joke here is that if everyone is above average, *no one* is above average (because everyone *is* average). Pretty much every founder I've met has told me that she believes her agency is above average, and thus should get a premium price for the business.

Averages exist for a reason. On average, most agencies will sell for . . . the average. If you go into a sales process with the expectation that you will get offers significantly higher than the mean, you may be disappointed and you may end up turning down a very good offer.

The second caveat is that the factors that determine the value of an agency are well known, and all other factors are mostly irrelevant. Are you close friends with the governor of your state? That's great, but it won't change the value of your business. Do you have a killer four-letter domain name? Good for you, but that domain is irrelevant when it comes to the price of your agency. Valuations do fluctuate. Just like selling a house, if it's raining on the

[2]Are ALL Minnesotans Above Average?, Science Friday, The World, 11/6/15.

day of your open house, there's a big football game on TV, and three of your neighbors just decided to list their houses as well, you might get a lower offer than you hoped. Or the opposite might happen— you might be the only house for sale that month, and you luck into a bidding war between five affluent potential buyers. But insisting that your agency deserves only the highest valuation and focusing on irrelevant intangibles rather than well-known valuation factors is a recipe for disappointment.

HARD FACTORS

Generally, there are two types of information that acquirers use to buy agencies: hard factors and soft factors. Hard factors are quantifiable, known metrics. Soft factors are perceptions and estimates. Hard factors are almost always given more weight than soft factors. The hard factors below are listed in order of importance.

◼ HARD FACTOR #1: LTM EBITDA

The top hard factor that acquirers look at is an agency's last 12 months of **EBITDA.** This is usually referred to as either **LTM** (last 12 months) of EBITDA or **TTM** (trailing 12 months) of EBITDA. Both mean the same thing. Note that when this data is presented to the acquirer, it's broken down by month, so that the acquirer can see the trends in performance during this time period.

EBITDA is an accounting term that means "earnings before interest, tax, depreciation, and amortization." Without going into a multipage finance discussion, another way to think of EBITDA is simply as an agency's net profit. So, broadly speaking, if an agency brings in $10 million of revenue and after all its expenses ends up with $2 million in profit, that is basically the agency's EBITDA.

Keep in mind that this is not a calendar year metric, but rather a metric determined by the last 12 months of financial results starting today, whether that means January 1 or July 15. And remember, this is your last 12 months, not your best quarter in the last 12 months.

Acquirers will typically offer agencies a multiple of the LTM EBITDA. For example, an agency with $2 million of profit might be offered five times LTM EBITDA for a total offer value of $10 million. This is referred to as a "5X multiple," meaning five times the LTM EBITDA.

LTM EBITDA is the most important metric in agency M&A. It's a strong indication of the current health of the business. Using the most recent 12 months gives the acquirer a long enough time horizon to ensure that the data presented to them isn't an anomaly and also helps them see the most recent agency performance.

Agency founders are often surprised to learn that agency multiples increase as LTM EBITDA increases. For example, a company with $2 million EBITDA might get a 5X multiple ($10 million valuation) but a company with $5 million EBITDA might get a 10X multiple ($50 million valuation).

This happens for two reasons. First, a business with higher EBITDA is considered to be a safer acquisition than one with lower EBITDA. The assumption is that an agency that has scaled is going to be more stable and predictable than a smaller agency. In other words, size matters!

Second, more EBITDA usually means that the agency is less dependent on a few key team members for all of its growth. Small agencies may have a dynamic CEO who single-handedly brings in all the new business and manages the key accounts. This creates the "hit-by-a-bus" risk. If the founder or a key member quits, the EBITDA can disappear overnight. At larger agencies, there's less risk that the business is solely dependent on a few key team members. Later in the book, we'll discuss how to minimize this concern.

With the caveat that this is just one factor of many that will determine the valuation of an agency (remember: it depends!), here's a general range for valuations by LTM EBITDA:

- $0-$1 million EBITDA: 1X-2X
- $1 million-$2 million EBITDA: 2X-4X
- $2 million-$5 million EBITDA: 2X-7X
- $5 million-$10 million EBITDA: 5X-12X
- $10 million+ EBITDA: 8X-20X

To be clear, the range in these numbers is largely influenced by the other factors we'll discuss later in this chapter. But if your business is above average on every evaluation factor, expect to sell at the high end of the multiple range.

▣ HARD FACTOR #2: Compound Annual Growth Rate (CAGR)

CAGR refers to the year-over-year growth of an agency's revenue and profit. For example, let's say that over a five-year period, an agency has the following annual EBITDA:

- Year 1: $2 million
- Year 2: $3 million
- Year 3: $5 million
- Year 4: $5.5 million
- Year 5: $7 million

This results in a CAGR of the agency EBITDA of 28.47%. (There are numerous CAGR calculators online. There's no need to try to figure this out yourself!). CAGR is an indicator of the long-term health of the agency. It's also a good metric to determine how fast the agency is growing relative to its competitors. For example, if a **Holding Company** (Hold Co) has a CAGR of 12% over a five-year period, they will look to acquire agencies with the same or greater CAGR.

Agencies with greater CAGR are (not surprisingly) worth more than agencies with low CAGR. Because acquirers are paying a multiple of EBITDA, acquirers will bid more for a business if it looks like the future earnings are greatly going to exceed past earnings.

An agency with $10 million LTM EBITDA and a 5% CAGR over five years might be worth $50 million, but an agency with $10 million LTM EBITDA and a 30% CAGR over five years might be worth $120 million.

CAGR can be used to measure any key metric of the agency: EBITDA, revenue, and EBITDA percentage are the three most commonly measured.

◼ HARD FACTOR #3: EBITDA Percentage/Net Margin

EBITDA percentage **(net margin)** expresses EBITDA as a percentage of revenue. An agency with $20 million of revenue and $2 million of EBITDA would have 10% EBITDA percentage, or 10% net margin. Net margin is an indicator of the efficiency of the agency. An agency with a lot of revenue but little net margin may be bloated and poorly managed. In some cases, an agency with too much net margin is problematic to acquirers as well, because they worry that either the agency is cutting costs and delivering bad results to customers, or that the net margin can't be sustained.

Historically, Hold Cos have achieved a net margin of between 15% and 20%. This range is often used as a benchmark for the industry. Agencies that are below this net margin range will likely see their valuations slashed by acquirers. Hold Cos in particular are concerned about net margin as they don't want to acquire companies that will reduce their net margin (which will then reduce their public valuation).

As a result, they look for acquisitions that will be "accretive" to their net margin—either at or above their net margin performance.

◼ HARD FACTOR #4: Revenue (Real Revenue!)

If you follow Silicon Valley companies, you will frequently see companies go public with high revenue and almost no profit. And yet, these companies still command valuations in the billions of dollars! Alas, the agency world does not run this way. While revenue is important, it's really a secondary metric in the world of agency M&A.

Still, revenue is important. Strong revenue CAGR can sometimes be used to get a high valuation, even if EBITDA and net margin are lackluster. And an agency with low revenue and very high EBITDA can make an acquirer nervous.

One important point about revenue: media buying agencies sometimes attempt to include their pass-through media costs in their revenue figures. So, an agency that pays for $100 million in media costs (which is immediately reimbursed by the clients) and then charges the clients $10 million in fees might try to report its revenue as $110 million. Acquirers are interested in **gross revenue**, which excludes pass-through media costs (and influencer or affiliate payments). Net margin is calculated as a percentage of gross revenue as well.

◼ HARD FACTOR #5: Client Concentration

Acquirers get worried when an agency has a large percentage of its revenue or EBITDA concentrated in just a few clients. Imagine an agency that has 80% of its revenue and 95% of its profit coming from one client. An acquirer would be concerned about the potential of losing that client after the acquisition is complete, reducing the value of the acquired company almost down to zero.

Acquirers will often look at an agency's client concentration in a few ways. For example, they may ask a company to break down their revenue and EBITDA by percentage coming from the top five, 10, and 20 clients. They might also ask the same question differently by asking how many clients make up 33% and then 50% of the EBITDA/revenue.

The data looks like this:

CLIENT	PERCENTAGE	
Percentage of overall EBITDA by client and total EBITDA from the combined top five clients		
	By Client	By Top Five Clients
1	18%	18%
2	9%	27%
3	5%	32%
4	4%	36%
5	2%	38%

Generally speaking, client concentration hurts an agency's valuation as it creates a risk of catastrophic decline in valuation if top clients leave. As discussed later, this concentration risk could also impact the structure and terms of a deal, and acquiring companies will often tie client retention to total valuation.

■ HARD FACTOR #6: Project Versus Recurring Revenue

Some agencies sign multi-year contracts (or at least have multi-year relationships) with clients that have relatively stable monthly and annual revenue and profit. This is common for media buying agencies, who are charged with managing a client's media on a daily basis. Other agencies are project-based, getting paid to complete the project and then moving on to another client. This is more common in web development and web design.

Because acquirers care a lot about predictability, companies with consistent revenue and EBITDA are usually valued more highly than agencies with lumpy project-based revenue. Again, the acquirer fears that the big project the agency has this year will end and won't be replaced by an equally big project next year.

Of course, agencies with recurring revenue lose clients all the time, and agencies that depend on project-based revenue can show consistent, annual growth. At the end of the day, the actual performance of the agency is more important than the pricing model underlying that performance, but, as a generality, recurring revenue usually gets valued more than project-based revenue.

■ HARD FACTOR #7: Publicly Traded Multiples

The valuation of publicly traded marketing agencies directly impacts the valuations of privately held agencies for two reasons. First, they're indicators of the general enthusiasm about the sector. Like any industry, if investors feel good about the prospects of the sector, the multiple they're willing to pay to buy the stock of a company in that sector will increase. If investors are pessimistic, the multiple will decrease.

Indeed, investors don't even need to have a particular opinion about the agency industry *per se*. If investors are worried about a pending recession and all stocks decline, this negatively impacts the valuation of privately held agencies looking to transact.

The second reason multiples of publicly traded agencies impact private valuations has been already mentioned: Hold Cos always want their acquisitions to be accretive, meaning that they want to pay less for their acquisitions than what they themselves are worth. Thus, if a publicly traded Hold Co is trading at 8X LTM EBITDA, they're unlikely to buy an agency for more than 8X, and most likely will be looking to pay less. This is a strategy known as **multiple expansion** or "multiple arbitrage."

During the height of the COVID-19 pandemic, publicly held ad agencies who had previously been valued in the 10-15X LTM EBITDA range suddenly got valuations as high as 40X. This bump in public multiples trickled down to private valuations, with agencies that would have been happy being bought for a 12X multiple pre-COVID commanding 15-20X multiples during the pandemic.

SOFT FACTORS

Imagine getting a resume from a job seeker that's absolutely perfect in every way. The applicant has worked in your industry for 10 years, won numerous awards, has been promoted every six months, and has references that talk about the candidate like he is a saint.

You invite the candidate in for an interview, and it goes horribly wrong. The candidate shows up 20 minutes late, he seems totally disinterested in the interview, and he checks his phone every few minutes. He even takes the time to respond to text messages—and he can't answer a single question about why he wants to work at your company in particular.

These are all examples of "soft factors," unquantifiable factors that help drive a decision. When an agency is acquired, there are many soft factors that determine both whether an acquirer wants to make a bid for the company and how much that acquirer is willing to pay.

◉ SOFT FACTOR #1: Specific Expertise

Agency multiples can fluctuate wildly, based on the underlying services that an agency provides. Agencies get higher multiples when they offer services that a) acquirers think will be in high demand in the future and b) aren't offered by many other competitors.

A few years ago, I came up with a concept that I call *the arc of marketing channel adoption*. There are three steps to this arc:

- **No One Cares, No One Spends Any Money.** In the early days of a marketing trend, companies have no interest in learning about the trend and allocate no budget to it.

- **Everyone Cares, No One Spends Any Money.** In phase two, the trend becomes buzzworthy, getting featured as keynotes at marketing conferences and receiving a lot of press coverage. But still, no one actually spends money on the trend.

- **No One Cares, Everyone Spends Money.** In the last stage, the trend has been established as a legitimate marketing expenditure. Marketing teams allocate budget, but the hype has all but disappeared.

Agencies that offer services supporting the end of phase two or the beginning of phase three may be able to command a premium multiple, because acquirers see their services as being more valuable in the future. It's also more likely that large agencies haven't established practice areas in this stage of the channel adoption, meaning that more companies might be bidding for the agency, also increasing valuations.

Agencies operating in an established category (the end of phase three) may find that there's less interest in their business, either because the likely acquirers have already invested in similar services, or because there's a sense that the growth opportunity for the channel/service is limited.

⊙ SOFT FACTOR #2: Specific Geography

Geography can be a positive or negative, depending on the acquirer. Some acquirers would prefer to acquire only companies in their existing geographic area, perhaps because it makes it easier to integrate the agency, both culturally and operationally, or because they're focused on that region. Other acquirers only want companies that operate in geographies where they do not, as a way of building a global footprint that will attract large clients.

⊙ SOFT FACTOR #3: Specific Clients

Every agency loves to crow about their great clients, and every agency has a page on their website with a bunch of logos from recognizable brands. There's often a belief—I think largely mistaken—from agency owners that the quality of their client logos is a major factor in the price someone will pay for their agency.

This is mostly untrue. The primary factors that acquirers consider are the hard factors described in previous pages, in particular LTM EBITDA, EBITDA CAGR, and net margin. An agency with Coke, Google, Apple, and Disney as clients with $5 million EBITDA is worth less than an agency with no recognizable names but with $10 million EBITDA.

That said, there are instances where specific clients can increase valuation. First, if the acquirer has a particular interest in doing business with an agency's client, the acquirer may be willing to pay more. Let's say, for example, that a large agency really wants to do business with Coke. Acquiring a smaller agency with an existing relationship with Coke may be a way to "get a foot in the door" with the client.

Clients may also matter if an agency has a strong client roster in a particular vertical. A larger agency that wants to win business in the airline industry might buy a smaller agency with several airline clients. In the case of a strategic acquirer, that company's target client profile (for example, enterprise vs. small and medium-sized business [SMB] clients) could also dictate whether they're interested in a particular agency.

⊙ SOFT FACTOR #4: The Agency Management Team

The quality (or lack thereof) of your management team can influence how much an acquirer is willing to pay for your agency. If you've built out a seasoned management team, an acquirer is likely to have more confidence in your ability to achieve above-average performance in the future. A strong management team also reduces the "hit-by-a-bus" fear that if one key team member leaves, the whole company might crumble.

In rare cases, the management team is a more important factor in determining valuation than the financial performance itself. This might occur when a young agency that has not yet hit its stride is given very high multiples because the acquirer wants to "**acqui-hire**" the management team.

On the other hand, an inexperienced or incomplete management team is a liability that will reduce valuation. An acquirer looking at an agency that's missing a key executive (like a CFO) has to account for the expense of hiring this missing piece, which means that the actual EBITDA of the company should be less than what it's currently reporting. Holes in the management team also raise doubts about whether the agency will be able to scale. In fact, in such cases, acquirers often adjust the EBITDA they use for their valuation model to accommodate the increased go-forward costs associated with the need to bring in expertise. Conversely, where there are redundancies, sometimes the buying party will factor that in as a positive EBITDA adjustment from the seller perspective (the acquirer will plan on terminating unnecessary and expensive executives as a quick way to improve EBITDA).

POSITIONING YOURSELF IN THE SALE—IMPORTANT OR IRRELEVANT?

Because agency success is usually directly correlated to the strength of the agency's management team, acquirers are very concerned with keeping top talent at the agency post-acquisition. Acquirers will always assume the founder is vital to the agency's continued success, meaning that the acquirer will structure the deal in a way that requires (or highly incentivizes) you to stay with the agency for a period of years. For many founders, this isn't a big issue, because they want to continue running the business. If, however, your plan is to sell the agency and then leave as quickly as possible, you need to develop a plan and a story long before you begin the selling process that positions you as an irrelevant member of the team.

Acquirers will always assume the founder is vital to the agency's continued success, meaning that the acquirer will structure the deal in a way that requires (or highly incentivizes) you to stay with the agency for a period of years.

You can do this in a few ways:

- **Fire Yourself from Jobs**. At least six months before you sell, delegate responsibility to as many people as possible. Ideally this means appointing a CEO to run the business, having a sales and marketing team that doesn't depend on you to close deals and has the ability to generate leads without your network, hiring an experienced CFO, and having a COO who can handle HR, legal, and operations. Of course, make sure that the people who replace you are as good or better than you. Don't hire substandard leaders just so you can convince potential buyers that you aren't crucial to the future success of the agency.

- **Be Overly Humble**. The adage "Accept blame, delegate credit" applies here. When the acquirer asks you about your contribution to the company, make yourself seem as irrelevant as possible. For example, you might say, "It's true that many of our clients today came from my network and I led those sales pitches. But over the last six months, I've only been involved in a few pitches. Most of the leads for new business have come from our sales outreach. Our future growth is almost entirely the result of our sales and marketing efforts and has little to do with me."

- **Be Transparent about Your Intentions**. If you want to leave after the sale closes, state this upfront in all of your communications with potential buyers. For example, you might write a note in the introductory teaser that states: "Non-operational founder has hired a professional management team who has successfully run and grown the business and is looking for a buyer to purchase his ownership stake. Founder will not be continuing with the company post-close."

- **Be Willing to Sign a Non-Compete**. If the buyer lets you leave the company at the close, they'll almost certainly insist that you sign non-compete and non-solicitation agreements. Arguing that you shouldn't sign a non-compete is a big red flag to a buyer, indicating that you intend to sell your current agency and immediately launch a competitor. Note: Even in states like California, where non-competes are on their face invalid for employees, they're still enforceable when an owner sells her equity, so this argument won't pass muster.

◉ SOFT FACTOR #5: Tech or Services?

A multiple of LTM EBITDA is the standard method of valuation for agencies, but that's not the formula used to value technology companies. Indeed, it's not uncommon for tech companies who are losing tons of money (negative EBITDA) to be valued in the billions of dollars. Often, tech companies are valued on a multiple of revenue instead of EBITDA. And these valuations can be as much as 100 times revenue!

To put that in perspective, if you have an agency with $10 million revenue and $2 million EBITDA, you might be worth $10 million, but a tech company with $10 million of revenue might be worth $1 billion!

Given the vast difference between these two valuations, it's not surprising that some agencies try to sell themselves as technology companies rather than as agencies. Can this strategy work to achieve a higher valuation?

The answer, like everything when it comes to valuation is . . . it depends! First, to call yourself a tech company you have to build actual tech. Buying off-the-shelf software programs or having an IT staff that helps you get all of your data into the Cloud does not qualify you for tech company valuations. To be considered a tech company, you need to build proprietary software or hardware (for marketing agencies, it's almost always software).

Second, the technology needs to enable exponential growth for your business. Tech companies get sky-high valuations—even when they're losing tons of money—on the assumption that their tech will someday enable them to make massive profit. The tech may cost a lot to build, and during the building phase the company doesn't make money, but at some point, the company can bring on new customers at virtually no incremental cost per new customer. At that point, profits grow dramatically. That investment is reflected in a reduced EBITDA for the investment periods. Therefore, a seller will need to make the case that a buyer should look at a normalized level of EBITDA that accounts for the investment. This is often a challenging give-and-take discussion in the M&A context.

Thus, an agency will only get a tech valuation if the agency can demonstrate to acquirers that the tech it has built is someday going to create exponential growth, both in revenue and profit. That said, in these cases, the improvement in valuation is not exponential in comparison to the aforementioned Software as a Service (SaaS) valuations, but can add a premium.

Non-scalable tech can still benefit an agency's valuation. If an agency has tech that improves the EBITDA of the business, that increases valuation.

IN SHORT: IT DEPENDS!

Agency valuation is an imprecise and unpredictable game. An agency might sell for 10X LTM EBITDA this week, and a seemingly identical agency might get 50% of that valuation six months later. Sometimes the reasons for the differences in valuation make sense. Maybe the second agency lacks a seasoned management team, has too much client concentration, and has disappointing EBITDA CAGR.

But sometimes, there's no clear reason. It could just be bad luck. Perhaps most of the likely acquirers already bought up similar agencies, thus reducing the number of bidders for the second agency. Or perhaps worries about the stock market just made acquirers more conservative in their bids.

For agency owners, the best advice is twofold. First, don't get caught up in "whisper numbers" about the sales prices for other agencies.

Whisper numbers are often not true to begin with, and even the truthful reports are only indicative of the value of a particular agency, at a particular time, with a particular set of bidders. Selling an agency is not like selling a stock. It's an opaque, unpredictable, and sometimes irrational process.

The second piece of advice is to control what you can control, and don't worry about what you can't. You can control your financial goals and, to some degree, optimize how much EBITDA you make. You can invest in areas that you think will drive growth. You can hire talented leaders. You can go after certain types of clients. You can build a culture that delights clients and retains them forever.

In other words, you can build the best business you can. Everything else—public agency valuations, the number of acquirers in the market, whether acquirers think your service offering and clients are valuable—is irrelevant.

Focusing on your business rather than what you think acquirers want, by the way, puts you in a great position with acquirers. If you don't get the valuation you want, you can just say, "No, thank you" and continue to build a great business. Having a "walk away" position is a great way to get an acquirer to reconsider its initial offer and try to sweeten the deal with a better offer.

You may now realize that the metrics on which you've focused to date are not going to drive the valuation you want. In that case, the best thing to do may be to put your head down for one to two years and focus on the metrics that matter to a buyer. That will have a far better outcome than going to market with a price that's out of whack, burning bridges with potential buyers, wasting time, distracting your team, and hurting financial performance.

A buyer's interest in an agency and the price they're willing to pay are based on numerous factors, some quantitative (hard) and some qualitative (soft).

The most important factors are quantitative. This includes (in order of importance):

- LTM EBITDA
- EBITDA CAGR
- EBITDA Margin (Net Margin)
- Revenue
- Revenue CAGR
- Client Concentration
- Project vs. Recurring Revenue
- Publicly Traded Company Multiples

Qualitative factors often increase or decrease the value of an agency but are usually secondary in importance to quantitative factors. Key qualitative (soft) factors include:

- Expertise
- Geography
- Clients
- Agency Management Team
- Proprietary Technology

There's no precise formula for predicting the value of an agency, but there are generally accepted ranges that are largely based on LTM EBITDA as the guiding principle, with multiples increasing as LTM EBITDA increases.

WHAT'S YOUR MARKETING SERVICES AGENCY BUSINESS WORTH?

Ground Rules

1. Profitability Is King

Your profit, or TTM EBITDA, matters most to a potential buyer.

2. Use Relevant Comparisons

Use similar companies to yours to estimate your value.

3. Get The Full Story

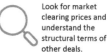

Look for market clearing prices and understand the structural terms of other deals.

THE GOLDEN FORMULA

ENTERPRISE VALUE (EV) = TTM EBITDA* X MULTIPLE

*Earnings Before Interest, Taxes, Depreciation and Amortization over the Trailing Twelve Months

TTM EBITDA	MULTIPLE	% of EV in Earnout/Rollover
<$1,000,000	3-4X	50%
$1M to $3M	4-6X	40-50%
$3M to $5M	6-8X	20-30%
$5M to $10M	8-12X	20%
$10M to $15M	10-15X	10-20%
>$15M	>15X	0-10%

This table is an estimate. Actual results will vary.

What Goes Into A Multiple?

LOW END (DEALBREAKER)	MIDDLE TIER	HIGH END
GROWTH AND MARGINS		
<10% Organic Growth Rate	10-20% Organic Growth Rate	>20% Organic Growth Rate
Net/EBIT Margins <10%	Net/EBIT Margins 10-20%	Net/EBIT Margins >20%
CLIENTS AND REVENUE		
Top Client Over 25% of Revenue	Top Client 10-20% of Revenue	Top Client <5% of Revenue
Mostly Project-Based Revenue	50/50 Mix of Project and Recurring	>80% Retainer/Recurring Revenue
<20% Client Retention Y/Y	50% Client Retention Y/Y	>80% Client Retention Y/Y
Clients Are Mostly Unknown Brands	Clients Are Mix of Unknown, SMB and Enterprise Brands	Clients Are Mostly Enterprise Brands/Household Names
SALES AND MARKETING		
Founder-Centric	Basic CRM and Pipeline Reporting	Robust CRM and Marketing System
No CRM or Marketing Automation	Sales and Marketing Teams	Sales and Marketing Leaders & Teams
No Sales Commission/Bonus Program	Founder Joins Sales Calls	Robust Commission/ Bonus Plan
FINANCE AND OPERATIONS		
Lack of Systems, People Dependent	Mainly Excel-Driven, Outside of Accounting	Documented Systems, Core Processes and Training For All
Non-GAAP Accounting	Reviewed Financials and GAAP Accounting	Robust Financial Systems
Inaccurate Gross Margins		Audited Financials
TEAM AND PEOPLE		
Above Average Employee Turnover	More Than 20% Contractors	W2 Employees In Majority of Roles
Contractors Performing Key Roles	Key Executives Have Meaningful Equity	Many Key Employees Have Equity or Deferred Compensation
No Equity For Key Employees	Basic Level of Benefits	All Key Employee Salaries At Market Level
Limited Employee Benefits		

© 2021 robertglazer.com

CHAPTER FOUR

WHO BUYS AGENCIES?

It takes guts to buy an agency. Think about it. An agency is just a collection of people. So a company could hand an agency founder millions of dollars and then see all the agency's value walk out the door. Imagine buying a house and then showing up at your new address the day after your purchase and discovering that half the house is missing!

Of course, buyers have financial and legal strategies to protect their investment, which we'll cover in detail later. Still, it's worth remembering that when talking to a potential buyer, this is a purchase that requires a lot of research and a big leap of faith!

Generally speaking, there are four types of companies that buy agencies: holding companies, private equity firms, **strategics**, and your partners.

HOLDING COMPANIES

A holding company (or a "Hold Co" for short) is a large company that owns many agencies. Think of a holding company as a large consumer brand like Proctor and Gamble or Unilever. These companies own brands across many categories (toothpaste, dish detergent, shampoo). A holding company does the same thing with agencies. A holding company like WPP owns hundreds of agencies across the world. Collectively, these agencies can basically do any marketing-related task clients require: online and offline, performance and brand, advertising and PR, martech and adtech, US and international, and so on!

The breadth of services is a major selling point for a holding company. In theory, a client can sign an **agency of record** relationship with a holding company and then work with different agencies owned by the Hold Co to handle all of their needs.

Traditional Hold Cos include WPP, Publicis, Omnicom, and Dentsu. Newly created Hold Cos include DEPT (the parent company of 3Q), Brandtech, S4, Jellyfish, We The People Group, and Stagwell.

Hold Cos are either publicly traded companies or are heavily funded by investors who expect them to eventually go public.

WHY DO HOLD COS BUY AGENCIES?

There are a few reasons Hold Cos buy agencies:

- **To Add a New Offering for Clients**. Again, because some clients want "one throat to choke," it's important for Hold Cos to be able to offer clients pretty much any marketing service or technology they can imagine. Thus, if a Hold Co is lacking a particular marketing service, technology, or location (or a combination of the three), they'll likely be in the market to acquire one of these businesses.

- **To Take Out a Smaller Competitor**. If a Hold Co sees a smaller company beating it for deals, it may buy the agency (either because it feels like it will uplevel its services by acquiring it, or just because they want less competition).

- **Financial Optimization**. Hold Cos are money-driven. Of course, every business wants to make money, but holding companies have the added pressure of having either public or private investors who are expecting a return. As such, they'll sometimes buy an agency simply because they believe they can profit off the acquisition.

There are two ways that a Hold Co might make profit off an acquisition. First, they may feel like the current management team isn't maximizing profit in the agency. By buying the agency and replacing the management with better operators, they can immediately drive more profit from the business. The second strategy is known as "multiple expansion." Small agencies are typically worth less than big agencies (as discussed in Chapter Three). As a result, if a big agency valued at 15X EBITDA buys a smaller agency for 6X EBITDA, the big agency can immediately add the smaller company's EBITDA to its EBITDA and increase the valuation of that EBITDA from 6X to 15X.

Hold Cos typically buy agencies that have already achieved some level of scale. This usually means that the agency needs to have at least $5 million of LTM EBITDA to be a potential acquisition target for a Hold Co.

WHAT ARE THE PROS AND CONS OF SELLING TO A HOLD CO?

👍 PRO: A Well-Managed Purchase

Hold Cos are professional acquirers. As such, they know how to manage an acquisition and have professionals who are exclusively focused on this. These folks are usually called "corporate development" or "corp dev" for short. So, in theory, selling to a Hold Co should be a professional experience that runs smoothly with few surprises.

👍 PRO: Post-Sale Resources to Help You Grow

Once acquired by the Hold Co, you now have access to the Hold Co's deal flow and the gravitas of being part of a multibillion dollar, multinational agency. If you want to grow your business, a Hold Co may be able to help you accelerate your growth substantially.

👍 PRO: A Clear Exit Strategy for Founders

Hold Cos typically demand (and incentivize) founders to stick around for between two and four years. After that, the founder can leave if he chooses, and his agency will continue as part of the Hold Co.

👎 CON: Aggressive Negotiations

Hold Cos employ an army of experts who are all trying to optimize the return on an acquisition for the Hold Co. This means that you're going to be negotiating against top-tier law firms, financial experts will scrutinize every aspect of your business hoping to find something that justifies reducing the value of the deal, and corp dev negotiators will push you on deal points right up to deal signature. All of this requires you to hire your own army of experts and negotiate aggressively, which increases your transaction costs and can be very stressful.

👎 CON: Culture Can Be Lacking

Many people in the agency world refuse to work at Hold Cos because the culture often focuses on hitting financial goals first and foremost above all else. This doesn't mean that you can't preserve some of your culture after a sale, but it does mean that your culture will only be retained if you hit the aggressive financial goals the Hold Co will set for your agency.

👎 CON: Politics and Bureaucracy

While it's true that Hold Cos can help agencies grow, it's also true that this is frequently a myth. Because Hold Cos often have numerous agencies that offer the same marketing services, and because the leaders of these agencies are often incentivized on their own agency's performance, agencies sometimes feel that they're pitted against other agencies in a Hold Co, rather than finding a collaborative environment in which all agencies are working together to stitch together the best solution for a client.

👎 CON: Deal Structure

Holding companies almost always defer a large chunk of a seller's compensation for several years, via an **earnout** (defined in detail below). Often these earnouts flash a big headline number that's virtually impossible to achieve. Unfortunately, it's also common to see earnouts end in litigation over how much the seller is actually owed.

TYPICAL HOLD CO ACQUISITION TERMS

Earnouts

Hold Cos almost always require agency founders to sign up for an "earnout." An earnout is a future payment based on either the agency's future performance, a minimum time commitment from the founders, or both.

A typical earnout looks something like this. The Hold Co makes a monetary offer for the agency—let's say $10 million. Between 50 and 70% of this amount is cash up front. The remaining 30-50% can be achieved over a period of time (usually between two and four years) if the agency hits specific EBITDA goals. This is the earnout.

The earnout usually requires the agency to improve its EBITDA during the earnout period to achieve the entire payment. Usually the payment is on a sliding scale. In other words, the agency still gets something even if they don't hit the full EBITDA growth target that would get them the maximum earnout.

A couple of things to note about Hold Co earnouts. First, the calculation of the EBITDA generated can be tricky. For example, let's say the acquired agency jointly pitches and wins a new account with another agency under the Hold Co umbrella. To win the deal, the Hold Co promises the client that they'll only charge 2% of media spend to manage all the paid media—the stuff that the newly acquired agency will manage—and then they'll charge $250,000 a month for creative services—the stuff the other Hold Co agency will manage.

The total fee is $300,000/month. A month into the relationship, the Hold Co is making $100,000/month in profit on the account, but because they discounted the paid media to win the business, the newly acquired agency is losing money servicing the paid media. As a result, this new client is a win for the Hold Co, but is hurting the acquired agency's ability to reach its full earnout payment.

Second, remember that Hold Cos acquire a lot of agencies, so it's possible there are multiple new agencies in a Hold Co simultaneously trying to maximize EBITDA for their earnout. As you can imagine, this can create a zero sum game, where everyone is fighting for their piece of the EBITDA, rather than what's right for the client.

Third, you may be required to drop a large client due to a conflict of interest inside the Hold Co. If you are working with Pepsi, but the Hold Co's biggest client is Coke, the Hold Co may insist that you terminate your relationship. If Pepsi drives a large amount of your EBITDA, you may suddenly be much further from maximizing the earnout than you had anticipated.

In general, a best practice with earnouts is to limit their duration and define the terms as clearly as possible. For example, rather than a five-year earnout, seek a 12- to 18-month earnout. Seek to keep your agency finances completely separated from other parts of the Hold Co until the earnout is paid. Of course, this sort of short-term, "me first" thinking is the exact opposite of the synergies that are supposed to happen as a result of an acquisition. As the seller, you need to make sure you maximize your total payment, and poorly structured earnouts can cost you millions of dollars.

The first time I sold 3Q Digital, the deal was structured as a 45% cash up front and 55% based on an earnout. We agreed to a three-year "lump sum" earnout (we didn't get paid anything until the end of the three-year term), but insisted that we keep our books completely separate from the buyer, and that we had full control over which clients we took on, how much we charged, and who we hired or fired.

The earnout was aggressive. To get our full payment, we needed to double our revenue in three years. Perhaps the buyer didn't anticipate we would ever hit 100% of the earnout, but by the end of the second year of the deal, it was clear we were going to get there. The buyer was caught flat-footed and informed us that they weren't prepared to pay us what we were due. After numerous rounds of negotiations, lawyer meetings, and sweaty palms, we agreed to buy ourselves back from the acquirer (using the earnout amount due as a large part of the payment to buy the company back). Rather than getting the payment three years after the deal closed, we had to wait an additional year (we sold the company a year later and the proceeds of that deal more than paid for the earnout).

In hindsight, I'm glad we kept control of the business during the earnout. That made it easier to hit our earnout goals, and it also made it easy to buy the company back without a lot of HR and finance work. In the future, however, I would not agree to a lump sum payment many years after the deal was closed, but would have insisted on annual installments. This would have enabled us to de-risk and also discover earlier that our buyer wasn't able to pay us our full earnout.

Minimum Time Commitments

To ensure that newly acquired talent doesn't walk out the door, Hold Cos will sometimes require key employees of an acquired agency to stick around for a minimum number of years. This can be done in two ways. First, the Hold Co can create a time-based earnout. For example, the Hold Co might stipulate that if the top five employees of the agency stay employed with the Hold Co for two years after the merger, they'll each receive a bonus payment. The second way to enforce this is to require key employees to sign non-compete agreements. In this scenario, the employee is barred from working at a similar company for a period of time, sometimes measured from the date of the acquisition and sometimes from the date the employee leaves the acquired agency.

In some cases, the earnout is a combination of performance and time commitments.

As noted, the culture at large Hold Cos (and, frankly, most large companies) is usually a lot stiffer, more finance-focused, and slower moving than that of a small, entrepreneurial agency. If you thrive on living on the edge of innovation, failing fast, and putting culture ahead of profits, it may be very hard for you to stick around a Hold Co for more than a few months. Some entrepreneurs who've sold to Hold Cos find that the cultural mismatch is so great that the time commitment to get their earnout is worth foregoing just to get out of the Hold Co!

If you thrive on living on the edge of innovation, failing fast, and putting culture ahead of profits, it may be very hard for you to stick around a Hold Co for more than a few months.

FINAL THOUGHTS ABOUT HOLD COS

Hold Cos are big, money-focused machines. They work with some of the greatest brands in the world and often produce amazing, award-winning work. They're also prone to in fighting and heavy focus on financial performance.

If you like your small agency culture—where people come before profits and success is measured in years and not quarters—you probably aren't going to enjoy Hold Co life. If, on the other hand, you want to work with the biggest companies in the world and work on complex, global projects, a Hold Co might be the perfect fit.

PRIVATE EQUITY

Private equity (or PE for short) companies are investors who buy a stake in a private company with the aim to turn around and sell their stake for a profit in the future. Unlike venture capitalists—who invest in companies that are at the "idea stage" and often have no meaningful business—private equity exclusively invests in businesses that have a track record of annual profits and growth.

One of the unusual things about private equity is that no two private equity companies are the same. Some private equity companies raise money from **limited partners** (LPs), which can include institutional investors and rich individuals, whereas other private equity firms have no LPs and are either funded exclusively by the partners or are part of a **family office** (where one rich person bankrolls the entire firm).

Some private equity firms invest in businesses with only a couple million dollars of profit, and others won't even evaluate a deal unless the firm is doing more than $100 million in profit. Some private equity firms apply a strategic playbook (a repeatable process to improve the business through competitive analysis, targeted acquisitions, and operations improvements) to every deal they do, while others focus exclusively on financial tactics designed to make the bottom line look better.

In other words, it's important to evaluate every private equity company individually, rather than assuming that the deal/relationship you get from one will be identical to what you get from another.

WHY DO PRIVATE EQUITY FIRMS BUY AGENCIES?

Private equity firms make money by buying businesses they feel are undervalued, increasing the value of the business, and then selling it to another buyer or taking it public.

PE firms that buy agencies usually start by developing a thesis on a sector of the agency space. They do research into market trends and decide that a particular set of agencies are going to increase in value in the future, and are thus good targets for acquisition.

The buy-and-build strategy that PE firms employ has created a number of successful large agencies, and driven significant profits to investors.

PE agency deals are either **platform** or "**add-on**" deals. A platform deal means that the PE firm is buying a mid to large-sized agency with the intent of also acquiring other small agencies later to make the initial agency even bigger. In this sort of deal, the PE firm may make a bet on the founding team of the platform agency and work directly with them to source and negotiate deals with other agencies. The founder (or a senior C-level executive) is expected to stay with the company for several years and help the PE firm eventually sell the agency.

The agencies that the founder and PE firm work together to buy are called "add-on" deals. In these deals, the add-on founding team may or may not continue to manage their businesses. It's often the case that everyone at the add-on agency simply reports to the founding team at the platform agency.

Knowing whether you are the platform or the add on is important because it impacts your future involvement with the company, and often determines the deal terms. Most PE deals are add-ons. If the PE has already bought a larger agency than yours, assume that you are an add on.

WHAT ARE THE PROS AND CONS OF SELLING TO A PE FIRM?

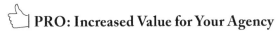 **PRO: Increased Value for Your Agency**

The first advantage of selling to a PE firm is that the firm is highly motivated to increase the value of your agency. Indeed, this is pretty much the only motivation that drives PE firms. This works out well for agency owners because, as we'll discuss in more detail later, most

PE firms require the agency owner to retain ownership of a percentage of the business after they buy the company. Thus, if you retain a $1 million ownership in the business and the PE firm increases the value of the business by 10X, the firm has helped you turn $1 million into $10 million.

👍 PRO: The Potential for More Flexibility

Unlike a Hold Co earnout—where a large part of a founder's payment is based on the founder staying at her agency for a number of years and achieving specific financial goals—most private equity **rollover** deals require neither a minimum time commitment nor a financial outcome for the founder to realize the total value of her equity.

It's sometimes the case that a founder sells to a PE firm and leaves the agency immediately upon the deal closing. In other cases, the founder transitions to a board or advisory role and is able to diminish the amount of time he puts into the company and work on other projects.

Of course, the founder has a strong incentive to keep creating value for the business: the value of his rollover (a percentage of a founder's stock that must be reinvested in the business after the PE firm acquisition is complete. This will be described in more detail later). So while it may sound amazing to be able to leave when you want and still get paid, the reality is that most founders want to continue to be involved in the business if their contribution will increase the sale price for the business in the future. Founders may be able to mitigate this concern by bringing in professional management (thus enabling them to move on without hurting the value of the business).

The involvement of the founder post-acquisition varies dramatically by agency. Still, as a general rule, rollovers offer more flexibility to founders than earnouts.

👍 PRO: Savvy Use of Leverage and Financial Optimization

Another advantage to working with a PE firm is that they're financial experts. While most agency owners know how to balance the books every month and pay payroll taxes, few know how to use money to make money.

The best example of this is the use of leverage. Leverage means borrowing money against the historical profit of the agency. Let's say your agency did $5 million in LTM EBITDA. Upon closing the acquisition, the private equity firm might borrow $15 million (three times leverage) from a bank against the profits of your agency.

They then take this money and invest it into the business, often into acquisitions that they add on to your agency. They do this because this is a very cheap way of growing your agency. Let's use some real numbers to explain how this works.

Let's assume that the $15 million that the private equity firm borrows against your $5 million LTM EBITDA is used to buy another agency with $3 million LTM EBITDA (a 5X multiple). The interest rate on this loan is 8%. The cost to "service" that debt (pay the monthly interest payments) is $1.2 million per year. Remember, however, that this acquired agency is making $3 million a year in profit, which translates to $250,000 a month. In other words, the monthly profit from the acquired agency is more than paying for the loan payments! On top of that, there's the possibility of multiple expansion (now that the combined businesses are doing $8 million instead of $5 million LTM EBITDA, the multiple an acquirer might pay could increase). So this can end up as a huge financial windfall.

Here's how this looks numerically (assuming an increase in the EBITDA multiple from 5X to 7X):

TABLE 4-I: Leverage Scenario	
Company EBITDA	$5,000,000
Current Valuation (5X EBITDA)	$25,000,000
Amount Borrowed (3X EBITDA)	$15,000,000
Debt Interest Rate	8%
Annual Debt Payment	($1,200,000)

Price of "Add On" Acquisition Bought with Leveraged EBITDA	($15,000,000)
EBITDA of Add On Company	$3,000,000
EBITDA Multiple Paid	5

Combined EBITDA Multiple of Two Companies	7
EBITDA Less Debt Payments	$6,800,000
Sales Price of Combined Companies (7X - multiple increased due to increased scale)	$47,600,000
Paying Back Loan in Full	$(15,000,000)
Total Return	$32,600,000
Contribution of Leverage to Investor Return on Sale	**$7,600,000**

👍 PRO: Predictable Timeline for an Exit

A fourth advantage of selling to a PE firm is that they have a finite window in which they will hold your business until they sell it again.

PE firms usually raise funds from outside investors (LPs). These funds are illiquid, meaning that the investors cannot withdraw their money whenever they want, like a public stock or a savings account. But there's an expectation that the investors will get their money back somewhere between six and ten years after the fund closes.

As a result, PE firms invest in agencies with the expectation that they'll sell them in no more than 10 years. In some instances, the plan may be to sell the agency in as little as two years. The average is probably a three- to four-year **holding period** (the amount of time the PE firm owns the agency).

The advantage of this approach is that the PE firm is incented to quickly maximize the value of the agency. PE firms are always "on the clock" and will operate with a sense of urgency. For an agency owner, it can also create a sense of predictability, knowing that the agency is going to be sold in the near future.

👍 PRO: Use of a Strategic Playbook

Lastly, some private equity firms have developed playbooks on how to grow businesses. This means that as soon as you sell to one of these PE firms, they have a proven plan for how to improve your business. This can include strategic hires, targeted add-on acquisitions, developing new revenue streams, and so on. Great PE firms "wash and repeat" with proven success tactics that improve every business they acquire.

> *Every PE firm will tell you that providing strategic direction to their portfolio companies is a key element of their success. It's not a very compelling pitch to tell a seller, "Sell to me. I'll cut 25% of your staff and increase your prices by 20%, and then pocket the difference!"*

A word of caution: Every PE firm will tell you that providing strategic direction to their portfolio companies is a key element of their success. It's not a very compelling pitch to tell a seller, "Sell to me. I'll cut 25% of your staff and increase your prices by 20%, and then pocket the difference!" Buyers know that sellers want to partner with a buyer who will bring fresh ideas, and so every PE firm positions themselves as a strategic partner.

The key to finding a PE firm that's truly strategic is to ask them to present their hypothesis for why they want to buy your agency. What specific trends excite them? Do they have specific add-ons that they have already identified that they want to combine with your business? What are the three to five things outside of financial optimization that they always do with their portfolio companies after acquisition?

 CON: Non-Financial Objectives Get Second Fiddle

Now, for the downside. First, because PE firms are only incentivized to drive increased value for their LPs, this can result in a disregard for non-financial objectives that might be important to you, such as culture, giving back to the community, or long-term investments. This doesn't mean that PE firms don't care about these issues. It simply means that they have to drive return on investment (ROI) for their LPs above all else, which means that sometimes these other goals will take a backseat. As noted above, every PE firm is different. Doing strong due diligence on a potential PE buyer will help you understand whether there's a cultural fit.

 CON: Leverage Can Be Risky

Second, sometimes using leverage on EBITDA can backfire. The doomsday scenario is when a PE firm is very aggressive with leverage, and the business performance declines precipitously.

ToysRus was purchased by several PE firms in 2005 for $6.6 billion. The company was profitable when purchased, and the PE firms heavily leveraged the business. Then—due to competition from online stores like Amazon—the company started to lose money. A lot of money. In 2017, ToysRus lost $164 million and had to pay $400 million in debt payments on top of that. The company filed bankruptcy in 2018.

👎 CON: Time Pressure to Sell

Lastly, the finite holding period of a PE firm can also be a negative. PE firms don't care about investing in strategies that are going to drive record-breaking results in 15 years. The PE firm must return profits to LPs quickly, and thus their focus is always on short-term results.

Not only does this sometimes hurt an agency's ability to make long-term investments, it also may end up reducing the potential price the agency could achieve when sold. Imagine, for example, that a PE firm has held an agency for six years, and it's in fact the last investment of the PE's fund (e.g., once they sell the agency, they can close the fund and move on to raising another fund).

The agency's founder has a high degree of confidence that she can drive 3X more annual profit over the next two years, resulting in a massive increase in the valuation of the agency. But the PE firm's LPs are clamoring for their money back, so the PE firm decides to sell now, missing out on a lot of potential upside.

To be clear, PE firms don't have to adhere to a strict timeline, and they aren't dumb! If the PE sees an opportunity for an amazing return outside of the time horizon that they pitched their LPs, most will give the company more time to maximize the return.

It's also worth discussing a sales timeline when interviewing potential PE buyers and making sure their timeline aligns with yours. If you want to cash out entirely in 12 months, it's unlikely you'll find a PE firm that's interested in such a short timeline. By contrast, if you hope to spend the next 15 years investing in your agency before a sale, you will also be hard pressed to find a PE sponsor who can wait that long.

TYPICAL PE ACQUISITION TERMS

There are three terms that are central to PE acquisitions that differ significantly from Hold Co terms.

The first is that PE firms usually require agency owners to "roll" or "rollover" some of their equity. Here's how this works. The PE firm makes a monetary offer for your business—let's say the offer is $10 million. They'll then require that you take a percentage of this offer and invest it back into the agency. So, if they want you to "roll" 30% of the offer back into the business, this means getting $7 million in cash up front and reinvesting $3 million back into the company. Note that this investment of stock back into the business is tax-free at the time of the transaction (Amazingly, there are some transactions where no money changes hands, and the IRS still considers them taxable events! A rollover is not one of these, fortunately.)

PE firms do this because they want founders to be invested in the future success of the agency. Think of this as insurance against buying an agency and having the founder immediately resign and retire on the beach. The percentage of the rollover is always negotiable, but is usually between 30 and 40% of the total deal value.

The second term is **preferred stock**. Not all stock is created equal! Most people who work at a company are given "common" stock, which is the standard stock issued to employees. Most founders (and sometimes key management team members) should insist that they get the type of stock that the PE firm insists on having: preferred stock. Preferred stock has a few big advantages over common stock:

- **Preferred Stock Gets Paid First**. Let's say a company sells for $5 million and there's $4 million of preferred stock outstanding and $4 million of common stock outstanding. The payout would be as follows: preferred stock would get $4 million, and common stock would be $1 million. In some instances, the preferred stock could get paid *all* the proceeds of a transaction and the common stock would get nothing.

- **Preferred Stock Gets Preferred Returns**. Basically this means that preferred stock gets a guaranteed annual return, paid out in additional debt or in more stock. This is known as a PIK, or payment in kind. Typically this ranges from 8% to 10% per year. Using the prior example, let's say that there's $4 million of preferred and $4 million of common and that the preferred stock gets a 10% annual return and the company has been owned for two years. So now that $4 million of preferred is actually owed $4.84 million, meaning that the common stockholders only get $26,000 out of the $5 million transaction.

Third, the PE firm gets additional fees. It's common for a PE firm to insist on an annual fee paid by the company to the PE firm. This fee operates like a consulting fee, It's not designed to pay for expenses like airplane travel or legal fees (these are reimbursed separately), but rather as a way to pay the PE firm for all the strategic and financial work the firm is doing on behalf of the agency. This fee is often a percentage of annual EBITDA, perhaps 2-4%. So a $5 million EBITDA company might pay its PE firm between $100,000 and $200,000 a year in **management fees**.

If you complete an acquisition, the PE firm may also get a deal fee for its work on the acquisition. Depending on the size of the company being acquired, this fee can be substantial (over $1 million for large deals).

It might sound like these fees are a form of "double dipping" by the PE firm. After all, the PE firm owns the majority of the business, shouldn't they be doing lots of work for the agency simply because they want to increase the value of their equity?

A great PE partner will put in a lot of work to help the business. This can range from identifying and negotiating add-on acquisitions, providing financial consulting to the agency's finance team, recruiting and hiring new executives, introducing potential clients to the sales team, developing a multi-year strategic plan, and eventually selling the agency.

FAMILY OFFICES

Most PE firms are funded by outside LPs who expect a return on their investment in a relatively short time—usually less than 10 years. There's a flavor of private equity known as a family office, which has no outside LPs.

For very rich families (usually at least $500 million or more of net worth), it makes more financial sense to build an internal investment team rather than partnering with outside wealth management firms. This internal group of investment professionals who are fully dedicated to investing the family's money is known as a family office. Many family offices have their own private equity unit, staffed with people who used to work at traditional PE firms.

The fact that a family office doesn't have outside LPs is a very important point when considering selling to this group. The big advantage is that a family office has no time pressure to sell your business. Whereas a traditional PE firm will look to flip an investment somewhere in the three- to eight-year holding range, a family office may decide to hold your business for decades. This gives the family office more flexibility than a standard PE firm. If your business is a rocket ship with massive growth ahead of it, holding onto the business can mean maximizing returns for both the PE and you.

Of course, this can also be a disadvantage. If you were hoping to cash out of the business in five years and the family office wants to hold your business for 20, you could find yourself illiquid with limited means of getting your cash. In some instances, you may be able to sell your shares back to the family office, but you may have to sell at a discounted price.

The other factor to consider when selling to a family office is that the family who owns the family office has outsized influence on your company strategy and eventual exit. A traditional PE firm has multiple general partners, so there are multiple opinions that matter. In a family office, there might be just one person who dictates the investment strategy. If this person is aligned with your ideas, this is great. If they're not, your life could become challenging very quickly!

FINAL THOUGHTS ABOUT PE FIRMS

Put simply, PE firms are lean, mean, profit making machines. Their *raison d'etre* is to drive a return for their LPs, which in turn gets them paid a lot of money! This is not to say that PE firms don't care about you, your employees, or your clients. But just as you have to keep your clients happy or go out of business, PE firms have the same pressure, and the only metric with which they're judged is the profit they deliver back to their LPs. Sometimes this creates great alignment and outsized returns for everyone involved. Sometimes this creates short-term thinking and aggressive decision making that can ruin a once profitable business.

As noted, PE firms run the gamut in terms of their strategic contribution, time horizon, deal size, and deal terms. Many are interested in the mutual success of both your agency and their fund; some are focused exclusively on their own enrichment. They're not created alike, so choose wisely!

STRATEGICS

A **strategic** is a company that wants to buy your agency because of a specific synergy they see between their company and your agency. Typically a strategic is not currently focused on offering agency services, but believes they can acquire an agency and then upsell these services to its existing customers.

Deluxe Corporation is a great example of a strategic acquirer. Deluxe initially grew its business by printing checks for businesses. As digital payments started to eliminate the need for checks, Deluxe realized it needed to offer different offerings to businesses to remain relevant. Among the more than 50 companies it acquired were several in the marketing agency space, including OrangeSoda (web marketing), VerticalResponse (email marketing), and Logo-Mix (logo design).

WHAT ARE THE PROS AND CONS OF SELLING TO A STRATEGIC?

👍 PRO: Strategics 'Get' Your Agency

The first advantage to selling to a strategic is that the acquirer usually has a specific need and strategy that your agency will fill. Unlike PE firms and Hold Cos—who may acquire an agency for its financial performance or simply to eliminate a competitor (in the case of a Hold Co)—a strategic is looking for a 2 + 2 = 5 combination. This often means that the strategic is willing to invest heavily in your future success and will actively facilitate integration with other parts of their business (unlike some Hold Co deals, where you might be directly competing against other business units).

👍 PRO: Strategics Might Pay More

In some instances, strategics will pay more for your business than a standard acquirer. Again, because the strategic sees specific synergy with you, they may be willing to pay a premium for your business.

👍 PRO: No Timeline to Sell

Lastly, unlike a PE firm, a strategic acquirer usually doesn't have a specific timeline for when they need to sell your agency. Indeed, most strategic buyers have no plans to sell your business or their business: they're looking for a missing piece that will make them stronger in the future. This enables you to execute on strategies that might be measured in decades instead of quarters.

👎 CON: Strategics Aren't Always Experts in M&A

Now, for the downsides. First, while there are some strategics (like Deluxe) that have completed multiple acquisitions, most strategics are not professional acquirers. As a result, deal negotiations can be a bit more bumpy than working with an acquirer who makes many acquisitions yearly. This may mean that the deal takes longer to negotiate—costing you time, money, and stress.

Indeed, early on in the history of my agency, I had two separate strategics offer to buy my company. On paper, both sounded great. I liked the management team of each of the other parties, and I already knew that we worked well together. Alas, both deals fell apart because neither party knew how to structure an M&A transaction.

In one case, I spent almost six months talking to a strategic about synergies and mapping out a go-forward strategy before we had any conversations about the price they would offer me for my business. Once they did make an offer, it was less than 1/3 of what I thought my agency was worth. A professional acquirer would not have spent six months talking to a potential acquisition without at least agreeing to a general range on valuation.

In the second instance, the strategic's CEO asked me upfront what I thought my business was worth. I told him a specific number. A few days later, he came back to me with a "heads I win, tails you lose" deal. He would give me the valuation I wanted, but only if I drove more than 150% of that number in profit over the next three years. This sort of low ball offer rarely happens when dealing with professional acquirers (assuming that they recognize that you are savvy about the acquisition process).

CON: Synergies Sometimes Don't Materialize

Sometimes the strategy behind the acquisition doesn't pan out as planned. The strategic may *think* that they want to get into the agency space, but then realize post-deal that their customers aren't really open to buying agency services from them. As a general rule, it's really hard to sell customers a new set of services beyond what they already buy from you. In other instances, the strategic may undergo a change in management that results in a change of strategy that no longer focuses on agency services. In both of these situations, the agency can sometimes feel like the ugly stepchild—suddenly no one at the strategic wants to care for them. This may result in a quick sale to a new company or a gradual winding down of the business altogether (and, if you have an earnout that's dependent on driving sales to the acquirer's customer set, this can cost you money!).

TYPICAL STRATEGIC DEAL TERMS

Strategic deals are often quite similar to Hold Co deals—the emphasis is on creating financial incentives for senior leadership to stay on after the deal and continue to grow EBITDA.

One way in which a strategic deal may deviate from a Hold Co deal is that it's not uncommon for the strategic to offer positions in the general management of the strategic to the executive team of the acquired agency. In a Hold Co, the agency executive staff is expected to stay within their agency, especially while the earnout is still being completed. In some strategic deals, the acquirer wants the agency management team immediately to take on a greater role beyond their agency, resulting in deal terms that incentivize the founding team on results beyond their agency.

It may also be the case that a strategic is open to (and may even prefer) to offer the agency a combination of upfront cash and equity, rather than upfront cash and an earnout payment.

FINAL THOUGHTS ON STRATEGICS

Strategics can be a great option for agencies. They may be willing to pay more than a Hold Co or PE firm, they see specific value in the agency, and they're usually very supportive of the agency post-acquisition. That said, strategic deals can often be hard to negotiate and sometimes don't create the synergy both parties assumed would develop post-acquisition.

PARTNERS

Sometimes the best acquirer of your business may be a person with whom you already do a lot of work. Your existing business partners already know your business well and likely have a good sense of how much it's worth.

This is probably the most common acquisition for small agencies— either because one partner wants to leave the business and cash out, or because the partners are no longer working well together.

PROS AND CONS OF PARTNERS

 **PRO: Less Due Diligence**

The biggest advantage of selling to a partner is that the partner acquiring your agency ownership stake doesn't need to do deep due diligence on your business. This can mean a much shorter sales process and a price that reasonably represents the value of the agency.

 **PRO: Less Disruption**

Another advantage of a partner sale is that the disruption to the business is minimal relative to a full-on acquisition from a third party. Assuming that responsibilities are divided up among the partners and the staff, one founder leaving the company shouldn't result in too much change for the average client, who will be sending checks to the same address, working with the same account team, and operating under the same contractual terms.

 **CON: Inexperienced Acquirers**

The cons of selling to a partner start with the fact that most partners aren't professional acquirers. Like selling to an inexperienced strategic, your partner may love the idea of buying you out, but have no idea how to structure a deal, do due diligence, or write the necessary legal documents to close the deal.

CON: The Potential for Conflict

The other con of dealing with partners is that M&A can be contentious and can strain relationships. In almost every M&A transaction, there are points where frustration and even anger take hold. If a deal falls apart, those difficult moments can carry forward and destroy what was a previously good relationship between founders. Just as some recommend that you don't do business with friends, the same can sometimes be said about trying to do an acquisition deal with a partner. As a general rule, the more money is involved, the more likely there will be conflict.

👎 CON: Limited Financial Resources and Low Offers

Unless you've already built a large agency that throws off millions of dollars of cash to the founders annually, it's unlikely that your partner is going to have much money to offer you for your stake in the business. A PE firm has deep pockets, thanks to investments from its LPs in the fund; a holding company (and often a strategic) sells its stock to the public to raise cash for acquisitions. As a result, these buyers can pay you millions of dollars upfront and value your agency aggressively.

This is not the case with most agency partners. In certain instances, the acquiring partner may be able to get a Small Business Administration (SBA) loan or raise some money from a bank to complete an acquisition, but more often than not, the partner is funding the deal with a combination of her own savings and the future earnings of the agency. With limited financial resources and a small margin for error, the offer you get from a partner is likely to be well below the EBITDA multiples a professional acquirer would offer. Then again, if your best offer is from one of your partners, it probably means that you aren't at a big enough scale to attract professional acquirers, and thus you should not expect those types of multiples.

TYPICAL PARTNER DEAL TERMS

Partner deals often rely heavily on structured payment terms over many years. This is because the average agency founder doesn't have enough money lying around to pay everything up front. Imagine, for example, that you have an agency that's generating $1.5 million of EBITDA a year and you believe the agency is worth $6 million (4X EBITDA). If you own 50% of the business, your stake is worth $3 million. Most agency founders don't have an extra $3 million sitting around to buy out their partner.

As such, the deals often have multi-year payment structures. A $3 million deal might be paid out as a $750,000 payment a year over four years. In this case, the agency is driving $1.5 million

EBITDA a year, meaning that each founder could take home $750,000 anyway. So the four-year payout is really just giving the founder her annual profit share. Still, it does enable the founder to focus her attention elsewhere, and get a few years of nice income, without bankrupting the agency.

SCAMMERS

On a regular basis, I get an email like the one below:

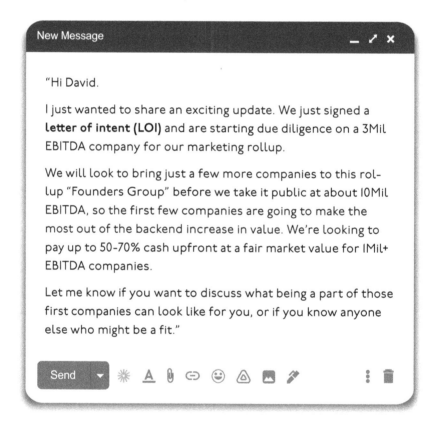

There are a lot of problems with this email. First, the email came from an individual, not from a known Hold Co or PE firm. Second, his claim that they plan to "take it public at about $10 million

EBITDA" is just ridiculous. Agencies need at least $100 million EBITDA (and probably more) to be able to pull off a public offering.

I don't think this email is a complete scam, as in, the author intends to defraud sellers of everything they own, like a supposed Nigerian Prince. What I do think is happening, however, is that this person is overselling the strength of his business and plans to underbid for any agency owner who contacts him. So an agency worth $5 million will get an offer for $750,000 from this buyer. If he makes this ridiculous offer to 10 agencies and one accepts, he's essentially made $4.25 million! He can either immediately sell the agency for the upside, or he can acquire a few of these and then sell them together, perhaps for even more profit.

This scam, by the way, is not just limited to unknown emailers. Big Hold Cos and some PE firms sometimes engage in the same "spray and pray" (or maybe, "prey") technique—mailing out dozens of emails, hoping that a small percentage of recipients will engage with them.

This is one of the reasons to hire professional bankers and advisors when thinking about selling your business. An advisor who has been in the space for a while has the industrial knowledge to tell you whether an inquiry you're getting is one that's specifically targeted to your business or is a bulk mailing.

As a general rule, if you haven't heard of the buyer, if the inquiry seems like it isn't customized to your business, or if the buyer is promising massive returns if you just "get in on the ground floor" (or a similar ploy), it's best not to engage with the inquirer, especially if you don't have experts helping you out.

- There are four main buyers of agencies: holding companies (Hold Cos), private equity firms, strategic acquirers, and your partners. Each type of buyer comes with distinct pros and cons, different deal structures, and different goals for the acquired business.

- Hold Cos typically buy agencies to increase their service offering and/or to improve their stock performance. The downside of Hold Cos is that their culture is often bureaucratic.

- Private equity companies buy agencies with the goal of re-selling the agency in the future for more money. They're experts at financial optimization. Private equity companies can drive outsized return for founders (who must roll some of the sales price back into the company), but can sometimes over-focus on financial return at the expense of culture or long-term investments.

- Strategics usually have a specific reason for buying an agency, which can mean that the strategic is willing to invest in growth of the agency post-acquisition. Strategics may be willing to pay more than a buyer that's solely financially motivated. The downside of strategics is that they aren't professional acquirers, so deals may move slowly. Sometimes their assumptions about the synergies driven by the agency are incorrect, resulting in post-acquisition problems.

- Partners are existing founders or executives who want to buy out a fellow founder. An advantage of partners is that they understand the agency's business already, so the chances of a post-acquisition mismatch is less likely. Partners, like strategics, are not professional acquirers, so the deal may not run as smoothly as a Hold Co or PE firm deal. They usually don't have the means to offer an aggressive price for your ownership stake.

CHAPTER FIVE

WHAT'S AN INVESTMENT BANK AND WHY DO YOU NEED ONE?

A few years back, I got a call from the CEO of one of my clients: "David, we've decided to fire your agency and do everything in-house."

Getting fired is part of life at an agency. What was strange about this firing was that it happened only three days after the company had hired a new CMO. The new CMO had never once called us to discuss our past performance (which was awesome), or our future strategy (which was sound). He had instead just unilaterally decided he could do things better than us, and we were shown the door.

No less than a week later, the CEO called me again. He started: "David, karma is a bitch!" He proceeded to tell me that the new CMO had made aggressive changes to the company's Google campaigns and in the process had violated several Google policies. As a result, Google turned off their accounts and banned them for life from advertising on Google.

Another way to summarize this experience: if you think an expert is expensive, wait until you see what an amateur will cost you!

Selling your company with an investment banker is like working with an expert ad agency. Deciding to go it alone can lead to the other scenario where you create a huge mess and potentially scuttle a great deal to buy your company. Investment bankers aren't cheap, but generally pay for themselves many times over.

WHAT DOES AN INVESTMENT BANKER ACTUALLY DO?

A good investment banker primarily does a few things: helps you prepare for a potential sale; identifies a pool of appropriate, relevant, and solid potential buyers; convinces potential buyers to submit high bids to buy your business; and helps you negotiate the best terms. Let's go through each of these individually.

PREPARING FOR A SALE

Like a real estate agent who advises a client to make cosmetic touch-ups prior to a sale, takes professional photos, and commissions inspections, an investment banker spends a lot of time "polishing" an agency to make it more attractive to potential buyers, long before putting the agency up for sale.

One of the first things an investment bank will do is clean up an agency's financial statements and associated schedules. Savvy buyers expect financial results to be presented in a specific way (more on this later), and an agency that goes to market with incomplete or unclear financial data raises red flags for buyers. This either results in buyers not deciding to bid at all or bidding at a reduced price. An investment bank will work with your agency's finance team to make sure that acquirers can easily read and trust your agency's financial data.

The investment banker will also start to prepare marketing material about your agency. This usually comes together as a **confidential information memorandum (CIM)** that's distributed to potential buyers to get them excited about the business.

Lastly, the investment banker will coach whomever will be presenting to potential buyers about how to respond to questions and generally emphasize the right points about your agency.

FINDING BUYERS AND GETTING THEM TO BID

Once your agency is ready for primetime, the investment banker will try to get the highest price from potential bidders. This begins by identifying potential acquirers and then reaching out to these companies to assess their level of interest.

Buyers that have shown enough interest are then invited to meet your leaders in person and potentially access more in-depth financials than what was disclosed in the CIM. The investment banker then sets a date before which all bids are due, to ensure that there are numerous bidders competing against each other at the same time. At this stage, the buyers will submit **Indications of Intent (IOIs)**, which are high level summaries of the buyers' offers for your business. Once the IOIs are received, the investment banker may play bidders off on each other, trying to increase the final price.

The investment banker will also help you decide which offer to accept. Because the banker has likely seen offers from your potential acquirers before (when representing other clients), the banker can advise you on how to value a given bidder's deal terms. For example, some buyers make aggressive bids just to get to **exclusivity** with a seller and then try to **retrade** the offer during due diligence. The investment banker can call this out and potentially avoid a bad acquirer choice for your agency.

NEGOTIATING THE TERMS OF THE DEAL

Once a buyer has been selected as the winning acquirer, the investment bank (in close coordination with the law firm, seller's tax counsel, and the seller's board), negotiates the terms of the deal. This starts with signing a non-binding letter of intent (LOI) that summarizes the main deal points and is the basis for the final contract (Note: As the seller, you may want to get LOIs from numerous bidders to increase your negotiating leverage. This will be discussed later).

Negotiating a contract can be a stressful and adversarial experience. Importantly, the investment banker often acts as the "bad cop" in these circumstances (as will your law firm). As agency founder, you can feign ignorance and defer difficult questions to the banker or law firm. This is important because the agency founder will need to work with the acquirer after the deal closes, so it's important to limit any personal animosity between the buyer and the your team.

Putting all of this together, an investment banker does several things for your agency:

- The banker brings expertise and professionalism to the sales process, increasing the likelihood of a smooth process. This is a "signaling" move that shows buyers that they can't pull a fast one on you.

- The banker creates a competitive bidding environment, increasing the valuation you get for your agency.

- The banker helps you understand the different bidders and the true value of their bids.

- The banker acts as a bad cop, so that you remain on good terms with the acquirer, even if negotiations are difficult.

WHEN SHOULD YOU HIRE AN INVESTMENT BANKER?

Ideally, you should hire an investment banker at least three to six months before you try to sell your agency. As noted, investment bankers need time to polish your agency's finances and create a marketing strategy for the sale. They also need time to identify potential acquirers.

Prior to a sale, the investment banker is also helpful in that the banker can field calls from potential buyers. Even if you aren't ready to sell, it helps to let inbound inquirers know that you have a banker and that someday you may be for sale. It also saves the founder time, since she can refer all inbound calls to the banker for screening and prioritization.

The one caveat to this recommendation is that some investment bankers charge a monthly retainer for their services (in addition to a **success fee**, which we'll discuss later). This retainer can be as high as $50,000 a month. If you want to work with a banker who insists on a high monthly retainer, it may be worthwhile waiting a little longer to sign with the banker (though don't be penny-wise and pound-foolish and wait too long!).

HOW MUCH DOES AN INVESTMENT BANKER COST?

Investment bankers make money in two ways: a retainer fee and a success fee. Sometimes bankers charge both fees, and sometimes they only take success fees, but they almost never take *only* a retainer fee and eschew the success fee.

A retainer is a one-time or recurring fee similar to an agency retainer. The retainer fee covers all the regular work an investment bank will do for your agency: reviewing your financials, talking to potential buyers, running a process, negotiating terms, and so on. It's also evidence that you're serious about selling your agency, and it's worth the banker's time to work with you.

Most investment banks would prefer to be paid a hefty recurring retainer for their services, but my experience is that this is highly negotiable. This is especially true if the banker sees the potential of a large payday from his success fee when your agency sells. In many cases, you can get the investment bank to charge a one-time retainer rather than a monthly fee. You can also insist that the banker credit all retainer fees paid against the success fee once the latter fee is paid.

A success fee is a percentage of the proceeds from an agency sale. Investment banks will usually structure this fee as the greater of either a minimum fee or a percentage of the sale. For example, let's say an investment bank offers you a contract that pays them the greater of $750,000 or 3% of the sales price. You sell your business for $40 million. In this example, the banker would be paid $1.2 million (3% of the sales price).

The amount an investment banker charges depends on the typical deal size the banker handles. A banker that handles relatively small deals (say, under a $10 million sales price) might aim for somewhere around $250,000 per transaction. By contrast, a banker working on $1 billion deals will expect $10 million or more per transaction. But as a general rule, most investment bankers don't get out of bed for deals expected to generate less than $1 million of fees for their firm.

Investment bankers are experts at negotiating (that's one of the main reasons you hire one), which means that you should expect a few rounds of negotiations when signing your contract with your banker.

Here are the main terms to negotiate:

- **Minimum Fee**. If you think your company will sell for $10 million and a banker is demanding a minimum fee of $1 million, you should either renegotiate him down to something much more reasonable or walk away. If the minimum fee is too high, you're either being ripped off or you're working with a banker who handles deals way bigger than you (as a rule of thumb, when it comes to both bankers and lawyers, you never want to be the largest or smallest client).

  On the other hand, if the minimum fee is too low, there may be a disconnect between the sales objectives of the founder and the investment banker. For example, if you would never sell your agency for less than $20 million, but the investment banker offers you a proposal at "2% of sales price or $200,000, whichever is greater," the banker is essentially telling you that he thinks the company might sell for around $10 million. When you get an offer for $15 million, the banker may be surprised and angry when you tell him you aren't interested in a deal at that price. A best practice here is to be upfront with your expectations so that misunderstandings don't occur.

- **Success Fee Percentage and Tiers**. There's a concept in investment banking called the **Lehman Formula**. The Lehman Formula creates tiers of declining percentages as a deal gets larger.[1] So, for example, let's say that a banker thinks your company will sell for $50 million. The banker may suggest the following tiers:

  - First $25 million of value: 3% or $750,000—whichever is greater

  - Next $25 million: 2%

---

[1] https://www.investopedia.com/terms/l/lehmanformula.asp.

– Next $25 million: 1.5%

– Over $75 million: 1%

If your agency ends up selling for $100 million, the banker gets $1.8 million ($750,000 for the first $25 million + $500,000 for the next $25 million + $300,000 for the next $25 million + $250,000 for the next $25 million).

These days, an even more common proposal from investment bankers is a Reverse Lehman Formula, in which the percentage of sales price increases as larger numbers are achieved. Again, if the banker expects a $50 million sales price, he might propose something like this:

– Up to $50 million: 2% or $750,000—whichever is greater

– Next $25 million: 3%

– Next $25 million: 4%

In this scenario, a $100 million sale nets the banker $2.75 million ($1 million for the first $50 million + $750,000 for the next $25 million + $1 million for the next $25 million). The argument for the reverse Lehman formula is that it creates an incentive for the banker to maximize the sales price of your business.

I've never accepted this argument, for two reasons. First, as pointed out in *Freakonomics* with real estate agents, when a service provider is paid a percentage of a sale, the incentive to truly maximize value is actually quite minimal after a certain point.[2]

For example, let's say that you have an offer on the table for $50 million and the banker gets 2% of that purchase. But your contract bumps your investment banker's fee from 2% to 3%

---

[2] Stephen J. Dubner and Steve Levitt, Freakonomics: *A Rogue Economist Explores the Hidden Side of Everything*, (New York: William Morrow, 2005).

for anything over $50 million. You really want to get to $53 million, which nets you an extra $3 million. That extra $3 million will only net the banker $90,000—increasing his take from $1 million to $1.09 million—not much more than his base fee. The banker is better off having you accept the $50 million offer, enabling him to move onto the next client with a minimum $1 million fee, rather than fight tooth and nail for an extra $90,000.

The other argument against the reverse Lehman formula is that in a flat percentage of sale agreement, bankers are already incentivized to fight for a bigger deal for you. If you have a flat 2% performance fee, an extra $3 million of deal price results in $60,000 to the banker. Thus, in this scenario, the increase in success fee percentage is only $30,000 more than what the banker would get with a flat percentage of sale agreement— not much of an incentive on a $1 million payday for him.

Ultimately, I would argue that bankers don't act any differently whether you offer a Lehman Formula, Reverse Lehman Formula, or a flat percentage fee. In each case, they're mainly focused on just getting you a good deal and collecting their minimum fee. For this reason, I strongly suggest avoiding the Reverse Lehman Formula.

- **Warm Parties Discount**. It's not uncommon for agency founders to have interacted with potential buyers prior to signing an investment banking contract. Because the investment banker did not work on identifying these potential buyers, you can argue that if a deal closes with one of these groups, you should get a discount on the banker's fees.

  This might look something like this: "If we sell to any of the following parties with whom we had prior discussions prior to signing this agreement (Company A, Company B, or Company C) in the next twelve months, we'll get a 25% discount on the fee for this transaction."

Bankers will likely object to this clause—in part because they just want the highest fee possible, but also because it legitimately creates a conflict of interest between the banker and the agency (the banker may push the agency toward a buyer that will result in a full fee for the banker).

In cases where the agency and a potential buyer have had meaningful discussions prior to the banker's involvement, however, a discount does seem reasonable and appropriate. This is especially the case if the banker's work on the deal will be significantly less than a typical negotiation.

- **Key Personnel Clause**. Agency clients are always worried about a bait and switch: The agency brings the A team to a pitch, but once the contract is signed, the C team shows up to do the work! This is also a concern with investment bankers. For this reason, you should insist on a clause that specifically names the people and team at the investment banker that will be working on your account. If the bank switches your team, you have the right to cancel the contract immediately without consequence.

  You may also want to specify that you want the senior people that pitched you to be active participants. This ensures that the investment banker doesn't delegate your deal to a junior person on her staff.

- **Beware the Tail**. One clause that you see in every investment banker contract is the **tail**. Here's how this works. Let's say that you work with an investment banker for two years. During this time, you meet with a dozen potential buyers.

In most cases, your investment banker has either set up the meetings or is there in person.

As your business grows, you realize that you've outgrown your investment banker. You terminate the relationship and hire a new investment banker. Three months into the new relationship, one of the companies you had met with through your old banker suddenly makes you an incredible offer, and you sign a deal to be acquired for $50 million.

Moments after the press release announcing your sale hits the wires, your old banker reaches out and notifies you that your contract with him requires you to pay him a success fee if within 18 months of terminating the contract with the banker, you sell to any company you talked to when he represented you. This is known as a tail.

Tails make sense. Because investment bankers get 95% of their revenue from success fees, it would be unfair to work with an investment banker for months or years, paying them only a modest retainer, and then at the last minute fire them right before you close a massive deal.

The question is: What is a reasonable tail? I would generally say that a period of 12 months is an average tail, with the range being between six and 18 months. You can also clarify what triggers the tail and what does not. For example, if your banker was at a conference and exchanged business cards with a potential buyer, that might not qualify for tail treatment. This level of detail can be important.

HOW DO YOU CHOOSE AN INVESTMENT BANKER?

*You never want to be the biggest or smallest
client of an investment bank.*

There are thousands of investment banks and they're definitely not all created equal. Here's how to find one that's the best fit for your agency:

- **Size Matters**. You never want to be the biggest or smallest client of an investment bank. Ideally, you want to fall right in the middle of the range. A banker that's too big for you won't give you the A team and a banker that's too small may not be savvy enough to hold his own against larger, more seasoned buyers. So ask all potential bankers the size of the last five deals they closed. If the number is far away from where you expect to end up, it's probably not a good fit.

- **Specific Experience Matters**. There are some investment bankers who do five to 10 agency deals a year. Among this group, there are some with deep experience selling performance agencies and others that excel with creative and branding agencies. A banker who has done a lot of deals that look just like your deal is going to know which acquirers to contact, how they structure their deals, and how much they're willing to pay.

  The first time I sold 3Q, I chose a banker who had just sold one of our biggest rivals to a Hold Co. The banker knew all the bidders who had lost out on that deal and who would likely not want to lose again (and thus bid more). We ended up getting almost double what we thought we'd get from the process.

- **Gravitas**. A recognized investment banker (or firm) is going to open more doors than one that's unknown, and this banker will have more connections to reach out to as well. Buyers also assume any deal represented by a highly regarded investment banker is going to sell for a top price, and thus may adjust their bids upwards as a result.

- **The Deal Team**. It's important to understand who at the investment bank will be working on your deal. Are you getting one of the lead partners or a young associate as your point person? How many deals are they working on concurrently? I was involved in a deal where the seller chose a B-level investment bank who put their C-level team on the deal. The process was full of problems, and ultimately the company didn't get a single bid!

  It's also important that you pick a banker that you like personally, or at least like enough to be "in the trenches" with him or her for many months. Some bankers are aggressive and ego-driven, while others are subdued and mellow. Both types can drive great outcomes for your agency, but if your personality clashes with theirs, you will either be miserable, have your deal fall apart, or both.

  Thus, it's important to be crystal clear about who exactly will be representing you. As noted, you may even want to list the names of the team in your contract and provide yourself with an **out-clause** if the bank pulls a bait and switch and replaces your chosen banker with someone else.

- **Typical Buyers**. Lastly, you need to understand to whom your banker typically sells companies. Some bankers have preferred partners to whom they like to funnel deals. This may be because they like the folks who work at the acquirer, or they feel confident that they're buyers who won't renege on a deal.

It's almost never the case that they're getting a kick-back or doing something unethical in preferring certain buyers.

That said, you need to know who these preferred buyers are. If they are companies to whom you aren't interested in selling, you may face subtle headwinds from your banker if you want to go in a different direction. It should be relatively easy to get this information. Just ask a potential banker to provide you with the names of the last 10 buyers to whom he sold businesses.

For an up-to-date list of top investment bankers who focus on marketing agency M&A, visit www.agenticshift.com/investmentbankers.

WHEN YOU DON'T NEED AN INVESTMENT BANK

In some instances, it doesn't make sense to hire an investment banker. Here are a few such circumstances:

- **The Deal Size Is Too Small**. If your selling price is under $5 million, hiring an investment banker will be expensive as a percentage of the sale price and most investment bankers won't even consider taking on your deal.

- **The Deal Is Simple**. If you received a straight-forward deal from a single buyer at an above-market price, you probably don't need an investment banker. Hiring a good law firm who has experience negotiating deals is probably sufficient. Of course, the definition of "straight-forward" is murky, so if you have any concerns that the deal terms might shift over the course of negotiations, it's probably best to err on the side of caution and employ an investment banker.

Even in these situations, going through a deal without an investment bank may still cost you money. For example, you may think that your deal is too small for a banker, but a banker may be able to get two times what you think your company is worth. Assuming you're too small is sometimes an incorrect assumption.

Selling to one company without running a process to elicit bids from additional acquirers often results in a below-market offer. Even if you think you've negotiated a killer deal, you don't really know what you would have gotten if the buyer thought there were other bidders involved. The mere fact that an investment banker is involved often gets buyers to raise their bids.

Note that some investment bankers are willing to take a discounted fee to work on a deal that's nearly finished when they're retained. For example, a friend of mine sold his business to a Hold Co. He was contacted directly by the Hold Co and spent a couple of months negotiating the terms of an LOI. Right before he signed the LOI, he engaged with an investment bank. Rather than paying the standard 2% fee, the banker agreed to charge just .75%. The banker then shepherded the deal through the LOI stage and closing.

WORKING WITH AN M&A CONSULTANT

One alternative (or supplement) to an investment bank is an M&A consultant. These consultants often come from large investment banks or are former founders with experience selling their agencies (I have a consulting business dedicated to helping agency founders in their sales process. You can learn more at www.AgenticShift.com).

Unlike investment banks, most M&A consultants charge primarily on retainer with a limited success fee. This creates a different set of incentives for the consultant when compared to a banker (who wants to sell your business quickly and for as much money as possible). Thus, the M&A consultant may help you in areas where the investment banker is not as useful, such as:

- Choosing your investment banker.

- Choosing your law firm.

- Providing another perspective on deal terms.

- Doing due diligence on a buyer's culture.

- Working with your law firm to negotiate key deal terms.

- Telling your team and client about a sale.

- Creating a seamless transition after the sale.

In some cases, you can use one of these consultants instead of an investment bank to complete your sale. In circumstances where your deal is expected to be at the lower end of an investment banker's range of deal values and is reasonably straight-forward, a consultant can be an effective and lower cost alternative to a typical bank (consultants may charge as little as $25,000 to help on a simple transaction).

In others, you may just want to have another expert on your side. Even if you have a great investment banker, you may feel more comfortable having an unbiased third party you can talk to during the process.

WHAT ABOUT BARNEY?

Barney (www.WeAreBarney.com) is an online marketplace for agencies. You have to submit an application to gain access to the site. Once you're in, you can list your agency for sale or browse listings of other agencies looking to be purchased.

Barney represents agencies selling between $500,000 and $20 million, though most deals seem to be in the $1.5 million to $3 million range. At this valuation level, most investment banks would not consider representing the seller because the fees they would earn from the deal would be too low (unless a seller was willing to pay $250,000 on a $1.5 million deal, which would be ridiculous). As such, Barney has entered the fray by offering a lower touch solution for smaller agencies.

I haven't listed an agency for sale on Barney, nor have I attempted to buy one. From talking to others who've used this site, however, my general sense is that the site can be useful, but that you should expect some bumps along the way. For example, an investment banker told me he had done **buy-side** work for a client and they'd looked into purchasing an agency they found on Barney. The investment banker expressed frustration that the financials they received from the seller were sparse and couldn't be relied upon. Given the small deal size, it didn't make sense for the buyer to invest in full financial diligence, and the deal fell apart.

The other thing to understand about Barney deals is that they typically trade at a much lower multiple than a standard agency sale. As noted, the smaller an agency's EBITDA, the lower the multiple. As a result, an agency doing $750,000 in EBITDA is likely to get a 2X or 3X multiple.

That said, deals do happen on Barney. If your business just isn't big enough to interest traditional acquirers or for established investment bankers to consider representing, Barney is a great way to connect with multiple potential buyers. It may still make sense to hire an M&A consultant, accounting firm, and a reasonably priced law firm to get your financials and your business story in order prior to listing your business. Beyond those upfront costs (and the fee that Barney charges, which is around $5,000 per month plus a 10% success fee), you may be able to sell a small agency on Barney without breaking the bank.

- Most agencies that sell for more than $10 million hire an investment banker to help them navigate the M&A process and maximize the value of their deal.

- Investment bankers manage the entire M&A process, including reaching out to prospective buyers, creating marketing and financial summaries about the business, scheduling meetings with buyers, negotiating LOIs and helping with contract negotiation. Investment bankers aren't cheap—expect to pay anywhere from $250,000 to over $1 million.

- Choose an investment banker that you trust, has specific experience with your type of agency, and who typically does deals at around the same size as your expected outcome.

- Alternatives to investment bankers are using an online brokerage like Barney (for deals under $10 million of value), and working with an independent M&A consultant, either to run the entire deal or to give you an additional resource beyond your investment banker.

CHAPTER SIX

HOW TO SELL YOUR BUSINESS

(Running a Process, Negotiating LOIs, and Choosing a Winner)

A few years ago, I got introduced to a PE firm by a friend. I was not actively looking to sell my agency, but I figured it couldn't hurt to have a quick phone call with the firm.

The call went really well. I felt that the firm really understood what we were trying to build, and had specific expertise that could add tremendous value. Over the next few months, I kept learning more about the firm, having additional phone calls and eventually flying to their headquarters to meet their entire team in person.

Over those months, I'd made the decision to sell the agency. Of course, I immediately let the PE firm know that I was going to consider acquisition offers. As I'd done in the past, I planned to run a "process," a structured sales process with multiple bidders competing for my business.

The partner at the PE firm asked me if I'd consider accepting an offer from them directly, without having to go through a formal process. I liked him enough to consider it, if the price was fair. I did a lot of research and came back to him with a number. We'll use $5 million for illustrative purposes only (that was not the actual number!). If the firm was able to create a deal at this value, I was ready to sell right away.

After a few days, the PE firm came back with an offer: $3.5 million. This was not the offer I wanted. So I told the firm, "Thanks but no thanks," and let them know I was going to run a process.

After only a couple of months, I received two offers that were between 20% and 50% greater than the $5 million I had originally proposed. The PE firm with whom I'd been talking then increased their offer from $3.5 million to $5 million, but they were now significantly outbid. I accepted an offer instead from one of the higher bidders.

The price you get for your business is not what you think it should be, nor is it the amount other companies like yours received. The price is whatever the market is willing to pay you. Running a process is the best way to get to this number and gives you the best chance of getting maximum value.

WHAT'S A PROCESS?

A process is a coordinated outreach, promotion, and negotiation plan designed to get you multiple bids for your agency. A process is almost always run by an investment banker. Typically, a process takes around three months to get to the LOI stage, and then between 30 and 90 days to go from LOI to completed contract.

CREATING A LIST OF POTENTIAL ACQUIRERS

A process begins by creating a comprehensive list of all the potential buyers of your business. In many cases, you can think of this list as a brainstorming exercise. Add anyone you can think might be interested in buying your company to the list for consideration. The list could include:

- Companies that have already reached out to you expressing interest in your agency.

- Agencies larger than you—in particular, holding companies.

- Private equity firms that buy businesses at your scale (regardless of whether they have bought agencies in the past).

- Competitors.

- Strategics who may need an agency to complement their other business lines.

It's not uncommon for this list to approach 50 or more companies. The investment banker will often create a spreadsheet with due diligence on each company's M&A activity and general financial health, as well as contact information for their M&A team.

You and your investment banker may then narrow the list down to a smaller number. There are two reasons to do this. First, the more companies to whom you reach out, the more companies will write back asking for information, and the more time you and your banker will have to spend talking to these companies. Of course, this is not a bad thing if you're getting responses back from highly qualified potential buyers, but if you reach out to companies that are unlikely to be serious bidders and they respond back, you're now likely wasting your time with a low potential bidder.

The other reason to limit this list is that the M&A process involves sharing confidential information with bidders. If you have included competitive companies on your list of potential bidders, you need to be prepared to eventually share sensitive information with these buyers. If you can never get comfortable sharing with a particular buyer (even after they have signed a **non-disclosure agreement** or NDA), they should be taken off the list.

SHOULD YOU RUN A FULL PROCESS OR A MINI PROCESS?

One important alternative to running a full process is what I call a "mini process." In a mini process, you contact a small number of potential acquirers—perhaps between five and ten. Each of these potential bidders is chosen because you have a high degree of confidence that they're great fits for your business—either because they've already reached out to you expressing interest (an inbound lead), or because they have a track record of buying businesses like yours.

There are a few advantages to a mini process. First, it allows your bankers to focus on a few great potential buyers, instead of casting a wide net and wasting their time with unqualified suitors. Second, it signals a level of professionalism to these buyers (Buyers will often ask how many companies have received the CIM. Knowing that you have already limited participation to likely buyers makes them feel like their time won't be wasted by moving forward in the process). And last, you'll be sending out your information to fewer people, which decreases the chances that your sensitive data will fall into a competitor's hands (Yes, companies sign your NDAs, but information almost always seems to get passed around).

One mini process approach is to limit the process to companies that have proactively reached out to you in an M&A capacity. There's a saying in the M&A world that great companies are bought and not sold. By only reaching out to people who've already reached out to you, you can plausibly tell bidders, "I wasn't planning on selling, I'm just talking to companies that have approached me." This gives buyers the impression that—unless they make a very compelling offer—you're happy to just walk away from the process and continue running the business independently.

You can also think of this by using Groucho Marx's comment, "I'd never join a club that would admit me as a member." When you run a full process, many potential buyers may think, "Why is this company selling? There must be something wrong with them!" In a mini process held exclusively for companies that contacted you first, this element of human psychology isn't a factor. Indeed, it can create fear of missing out and urgency!

SENDING OUT A TEASER

Once you have whittled down your list of qualified potential acquirers, you can send these companies a **teaser** about your business. This is a letter or email that gives the potential acquirer a quick overview of your business and asks them to respond back if they're interested in learning more.

The teaser will always conceal your business name and include a code name for the deal, like "Project Telephone" (the name of the project is usually random and has nothing to do with your business). The teaser is usually one page long, and includes basic overview information about your business: LTM EBITDA, what makes the company great, and contact information for the investment bankers.

Here's a (slightly altered) example of an email and teaser I received from an investment banker:

Hi David –

I am following up on an email I sent in July to see if there's interest in this opportunity.

We're working with Project Agentic, a full-service Amazon services company that provides automated warehousing, 3PL/logistics services, liquidity, and marketing services to over 200 brands across both Amazon (primary channel) and Walmart marketplace.

The Company will do $83 million of sales this year and roughly $7 million of EBITDA, up over 21% year-over-year.

Their business model is a combination of providing liquidity to over 200 small-medium sized brands (buy-sell) and also managing listings and ad budgets on Amazon for some of the biggest brands in the health and beauty space such as Unilever.

They have proprietary software systems to manage inventory and robotic 3PL technology and are seeking a capital partner / buyer for the business. It's 100% privately held.

I've attached a teaser and NDA if you're interested in learning more."

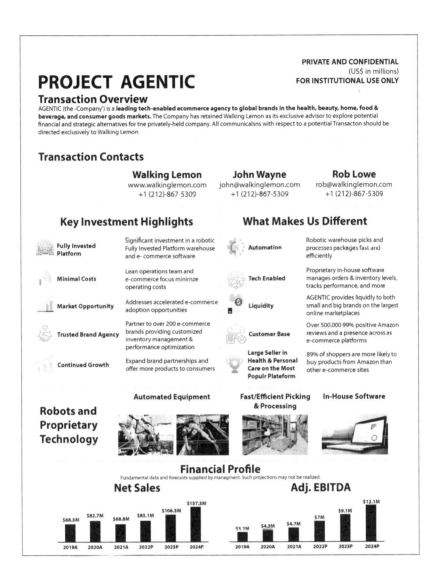

As noted in the cover letter, in addition to the teaser, the investment banker includes an NDA for the potential acquirer to sign. Once the acquirer signs the NDA, the investment banker sends out the confidential information memorandum (CIM).

CREATING AND SENDING THE CIM

The CIM basically takes the summary overview provided in the teaser and expands it into a comprehensive and detailed description of the agency.

Unlike the teaser, the CIM does not conceal the name of the company for sale (it would be impossible at this point, because the CIM needs to include the profiles of executive leadership, for example). A CIM is anywhere from 25 to 75 pages long and is usually delivered in either a PowerPoint or PDF format.

Common areas discussed in the CIM include:

- **Company Overview.** Company history and quick overview of the company today.

- **Industry Overview.** What are the current trends? Why is this an industry in which an acquirer would want to invest?

- **Summary of Services**. What are the key services the company offers? What percentage of revenue comes from each?

- **Unique Advantages**. What makes the company special? Descriptions of proprietary technology and processes. Product roadmap.

- **Customers**. Who are the top customers? How long have they worked with the company? How much of the company revenue comes from the top 5, 10, or twenty customers? What is the average revenue per customer?

- **Sales and Marketing**. What are the most recent new customer additions? How does the company win new business?

- **Client Services**. How does the company structure its team to support clients? Who are the leaders of this team?

- **HR**. What does the org chart look like? How is employee retention? What is the hiring strategy?

- **Financial Details**. A summary Profit & Loss (P&L) statement, showing at least three years of data and projecting at least one year forward. It should include revenue, cost of goods sold (**COGS**), and profit by channel, operating expenses by business unit (general and administrative, sales and marketing), forecast versus plan for the current year, and **adjusted EBITDA** projections.

As you can see from the list of topics, a CIM exposes a lot of sensitive information to potential buyers, so it's important that you have a strong NDA executed prior to sharing this, and that you only share the CIM with companies that are both highly interested in acquiring your business and unlikely to share the CIM with competitors. (Let's face it, NDAs are rarely enforced, so you should assume that your CIM will eventually fall into your competitors' hands).

You may even want to redact highly sensitive information from the CIM altogether. In particular, information about the names of your clients and the terms of your relationship with them (how much they pay you, what services you provide) can be used by a competitor to directly pitch your top clients. For this reason, it's common to mention "representative clients," which may or may not be your top clients in terms of revenue, but may be brand names that will impress an acquirer. You may want to only provide granular detail about your clients and services to potential acquirers that have made it past the CIM stage, and that have made you an offer you are strongly considering.

One other important point about CIMs. While it's OK to sell the "sizzle" of your business in the CIM by slightly exaggerating how awesome your business is, make sure that you don't make claims that are impossible to back up. Here are two examples. First, it's common for CIMs to show very aggressive future projections of profit and growth for a business. Acquirers want to buy growing companies, so investment bankers will often encourage an agency to put big numbers down for post-acquisition business projections.

This may indeed get an acquirer excited, but it also may get them to structure an earnout based on these numbers! And if the earnout is a large part of your compensation, you may be setting yourself up to never achieve the full offer value if your projections are unrealistic.

Similarly, if you exaggerate the significance of proprietary technology, you run the risk that a technical due diligence review by an acquirer discovers that your tech isn't that special. This can either skuttle a deal entirely or result in an acquirer "retrading" on the deal (offering you a lower price because of an issue discovered during due diligence).

GETTING YOUR FINANCIALS IN ORDER

Most founders shine at describing what makes their agency unique and how they provide amazing services to their clients. This sort of storytelling is an important part of the CIM. Where founders often get stuck is in presenting the financial story of their business in the CIM.

Recently, a friend of mine was approached by an agency looking to be acquired. The company, only a few years old, told my friend that they were booking more than $10 million of annual revenue—which was extremely rapid growth. He excitedly asked for more information, and was confused to see that the agency's EBITDA was less than $200,000, or 2% of revenue. He immediately set up a call with the founder, who informed him that the $10 million of revenue was actually $9 million of pass-through media costs, leaving only $1 million of gross revenue. My friend quickly passed—both because the company's growth wasn't what he thought it was, and because the company's management either purposely misstated their revenue or was too inexperienced to understand what they had done.

Having clean and detailed financials is crucial to maximizing the sales price of your agency and simply getting a deal done. Buyers can be skittish. Errors, omittances, or overstatements of performance are big red flags that will quickly lead a buyer to abandon a potential deal.

Having clean and detailed financials is crucial to maximizing the sales price of your agency and simply getting a deal done. Buyers can be skittish. Errors, omittances, or overstatements of performance are big red flags that will quickly lead a buyer to abandon a potential deal. Later, we'll also discuss adjustments to EBITDA. Getting these right in your initial financial package is also important to getting maximum value for your deal.

Ideally, you should engage with a team of experts several months prior to a process to help you polish your financials. Typically experts you'd employ to this would include:

- Your investment banker.

- Your CFO or head of finance.

- An external accounting firm.

USING GAAP

GAAP stands for generally accepted accounting principles. This is the standard way of recording and presenting financial data. Any savvy buyer will demand that your financial data be GAAP compliant (and, frankly, a company not using GAAP would be a red flag that would immediately disqualify the company from a purchase offer for many buyers).

GAAP accounting revolves around five key principles:

- **Revenue**. Report revenue on an **accrual**, not cash basis.

- **Expenses**. Reporting expenses on an accrual basis.

- **The Matching Principle**. Every item of revenue should be matched to an item of expense (this is also accrual accounting).

- **The Cost Principle**. Record the historical costs of an item, not the current value.

- **The Objectivity Principle**. Use only factual, verifiable data in your financial reports, not subjective measurements of value.[1]

If you aren't currently using GAAP, hire an accounting firm to review your books and become GAAP compliant. Note that this is not a simple task that a firm can complete over a long weekend. Plan for at least three to six months to get this project finished.

The first rule of GAAP is to use accrual accounting. Accrual accounting recognizes revenue and expenses in the month in which they incurred. Cash accounting recognizes revenue and expenses in the month in which money came into or went out of the business.

Acquirers want to see your data presented in accrual format, because cash accounting can result in huge fluctuations in financial performance. Imagine, for example, that you're presenting your LTM financials and a big client decides to pay you for 12 months

---

[1]Reed Phillips, with Charles Slack, *Quick Value: Discover Your Value and Empower Your Business in Three Easy Steps*, (New York: McGraw-Hill, 2021).

of your services in advance. If you're using cash accounting, your EBITDA would look amazing. Then, six months later—when your team is still doing work but the payment is in the past—your numbers would look terrible.

Accrual accounting eliminates this sort of mismatch between payment date and service date and gives acquirers a better sense of your actual performance.

If your financials are only able to be presented on a cash basis, make sure to note that methodology upfront, as well as any associated impact on timing of revenues or expenses. Note also that the buyer will likely make her bid based on GAAP EBITDA, which may be substantially different than what your cash earnings show (which means you may be disappointed when you see the offer).

CREATING A QUALITY OF EARNINGS (QofE) REPORT

Eventually, your external accounting firm will need to produce a **Quality of Earnings** report (also sometimes known as a **Sell-Side** Quality of Earnings report). Quality of earnings refers to the level of transparency, consistency, and reliability of a company's reported financial results. It's an analysis of the underlying financial and operational factors that determine a company's reported earnings, and assesses the sustainability of those earnings.

A QofE report attempts to present your financial information in an objective way. As shown in the prior example, agencies left to their own devices may produce financial data that's overly favorable or optimistic. Moreover, inexperienced finance teams may not be knowledgeable of all accounting principles and make errors—hence the need for an independent expert to help you get your financials right via a QofE.

A QofE helps you identify and correct problems with your financials before a potential buyer gets your data. This both speeds along the process and also adds confidence in your data. That said, sometimes in a process where the seller does not have a QofE report, the buyer will engage with a vendor on their side to analyze the seller's financials and provide an output of a QofE as well as a preliminary analysis of Net Working Capital (which we'll discuss later).

The QofE will answer such important questions for buyers as:

- Are there one-off events that have impacted financial performance?
- Is there sufficient working cash to operate the business?
- Is compensation in line with local and industry averages?
- Are real estate costs reasonable?
- Is the growth forecast reasonable?[2]

THE IMPORTANCE OF ADJUSTED EBITDA

A QofE also helps you identify add-backs and adjustments. One of the most important concepts in M&A is "Adjusted EBITDA."

Adjusted EBITDA removes one-time expenses and non-recurring items from your EBITDA. For example, let's say that your unadjusted LTM EBITDA was $5 million, but you had several unusual costs during that time:

---

[2]https://www.eidebailly.com/insights/articles/2019/2/quality-of-earnings-when-selling-a-business.

TABLE 6-1: Adjusted EBITDA	
	AMOUNT
Annual EBITDA	$5,000,000
Investment Banking Fees	$250,000
QofE Report Creation	$25,000
Wrongful Termination Suit Settlement	$100,000
Below Market Founder CEO Salary	($150,000)
Adjusted EBITDA	$5,225,000

Adding these adjusted costs to your EBITDA produces Adjusted EBITDA of $5.225 million. Assuming you get a 10X multiple on your business, this results in a net increase in sales price of $2.25 million!

Of course, there are also EBITDA adjustments that negatively impact the seller. This could include:

- Founders who do not pay themselves a salary, but expect to be paid at market rate once they're acquired. Entrepreneurs sometimes eschew full market salaries, preferring to get paid less than what they're worth and instead plow as much money as possible back into growing their business.

  There's nothing wrong with this strategy. That said, when it comes to selling your business, buyers won't give agencies EBITDA credit for the difference between a founder's actual salary and what the market-rate for that founder should be.

  After the company is sold, someone—either the founder or a newly hired CEO—is going to run the business. Many founders immediately ask to have their salary increased to market-rate after a deal is closed. Hired CEOs certainly expect to be paid at market. As a result, the acquiring company must take this into account and will discount a company's EBITDA if they see that the founders aren't getting paid a normal salary.

- Benefits that the seller isn't currently paying, but that the acquirer will have to pay (this is common in small agencies that have few employees outside of the founders).

- Vacations and personal expenses being paid for by the company.

Buyers will use points like these to reduce the EBITDA and thus lower the purchase price.

THE IMPORTANCE OF COGS AND GROSS MARGIN

Many buyers are interested in an agency's gross margins. Gross margins are calculated as revenue minus costs of goods sold (COGS). COGS is primarily the salaries of the account team managing a client's account, compensation for the sales team that closes the deal, pass-through media costs, equipment and benefits for the accounts team, and travel to the client that's not reimbursed. For example, if a client pays the agency $1000 and the agency pays the client's account team $300 in salary and spends $50 on travel and $100 on sales, the gross margin is 55%.

In some cases, an agency has low *net* margins because it's investing in future growth (technology, opening new offices, offering new services), but high *gross* margins because it's highly efficient at managing current clients. This combination can be a positive indicator for an acquirer and a reason to pay a greater multiple for the business, even if the LTM EBITDA is not great.

If, however, a company has both low net margin and low gross margin, it's harder to get excited about the company's investments in future growth. As such, a company that inflates its gross margin numbers by moving costs that should clearly be included in COGS to fixed costs is either ignorant of how to correctly calculate COGS and gross margin—which would raise questions about the quality of the finance team—or is purposely manipulating its financials, which is an even bigger problem!

Note: Some agencies don't bother tracking COGS at all, focusing instead exclusively on net margin and EBITDA. While it's true that EBITDA is ultimately the most important metric for buyers, COGS is also a core metric that buyers want to see—it demonstrates the agency's efficiency, and it's also a good indicator of the ability to scale EBITDA as the business grows. So even if you don't depend on COGS for your daily agency management, it's a good idea to have it calculated prior to putting your agency up for sale.

RUNNING MANAGEMENT PRESENTATIONS

After the CIM is sent out, the investment banker will reach out to CIM recipients to assess their level of interest. At every stage, it's likely that some potential acquirers will drop out of the process. Often, this has nothing to do with the company up for sale, so don't take it personally. It may also be the case that the investment banker and/or the founding team decides to remove some buyers at this point (For example, the potential acquirer might not have expressed enough excitement, or it seems unlikely that they could truly compete with the bids anticipated from other parties still involved).

However it happens, the goal at this point is to reduce the "wide net" of dozens of potential acquirers down to a set of more serious potential partners. This number could be as low as three or four, or as high as 15 to 20. It's partially dependent on how much time the agency's management team is willing to spend time pitching buyers, and how much confidence the banker has that there are enough bidders left to create a bidding war.

Pre-pandemic, almost all **management presentations** were face-to-face. Ideally, the investment banker would pick one location near many of the potential buyers (often New York, Chicago, or San Francisco) and schedule back-to-back presentations for the agency's management team. Now that COVID has made online meetings more common, it may be possible to hold some or all management meetings virtually. Although for a deal that might be the most important financial transaction of a founder's life, it does seem like making an effort to meet face-to-face is a worthwhile endeavor.

The management team presentation is a chance for acquirers to meet the agency management team, assess cultural fit, and drill down on items in the CIM. Typically, each meeting lasts between 90 minutes and three hours. In many cases, acquirers will ask the management team to join them in the evening for dinner, which allows for additional time to bond.

WHO SHOULD COME?

Management presentations should only involve the most senior, key executives of the agency. This is done for two reasons: First, because that's who acquirers are expecting to meet, and second, because as few people as possible at the agency should know that a potential acquisition is happening (more on that later).

As a general rule, I'd say that no more than six (and preferably around four) team members should be involved in the management presentation. At a typical agency, this list would include:

- The CEO.
- The COO or President.
- The CFO or Head of Finance.
- Head of Client Services.
- Head of Sales and Marketing.

- Head of Product/Technology (if this is a big component of the business).

MANAGEMENT PRESENTATIONS PREP

A management presentation is somewhat akin to a job interview. Think of the teaser and the CIM like a resume. The company has seen enough on paper to get excited about hiring you, but now they need to really get to know you and move beyond the "sizzle."

The bulk of the meeting revolves around the management team's PowerPoint presentation. Typically, this is not that different from the content in the CIM. If the CIM has 50 pages of content, the management presentation will probably boil this down to 20-25 pages.

The CEO/founder is expected to kick off the presentation, followed by subject matter experts talking about their particular parts of the business.

Preparing for a management presentation really consists of two things: First, you should know what you're going to say about each slide and practice your presentation many times. Coming across as prepared and professional can only help increase the likelihood that a potential acquirer will submit a bid for your company. Second, prepare for questions from your audience. Generally speaking, there are two types of questions you'll likely get during a management presentation:

- **Personal Questions**. Buyers want to understand your motivations and desires. As a result, you will get questions like: Why did you found your agency? Why are you thinking about selling? Do you want to keep working here after you sell? With which personality types do you work most effectively? How do you think employees will react to the news that you're selling the business?

- **Deep Dive Questions**. Buyers may highlight a particular point raised in the CIM or management presentation and ask for more detail. This could include: Why did your financials change drastically during a certain period? Why do clients leave you? How secure is your relationship with your biggest client? What would you say are the strengths and weaknesses of your company relative to your competitors? Why do employees leave?

One way to predict the questions that will be asked is to run a "red team/blue team" exercise. In this exercise, some of your team pretend to be the potential buyers of your agency.

One way to predict the questions that will be asked is to run a "red team/blue team" exercise. In this exercise, some of your team pretend to be the potential buyers of your agency. They then review your CIM and financials and come up with a list of questions they want answered. By trying to put yourself in the shoes of the buyer, you have a better chance of identifying the questions that will most likely be asked.

I asked ChatGPT[3] to come up with sample questions. The results were quite accurate:

- Can you discuss your current market position, including any strengths, weaknesses, opportunities, and threats?

---

[3]ChatGPT is a state-of-the-art artificial intelligence language model developed by OpenAI. Using the GPT architecture, ChatGPT has been trained on a vast corpus of text data, including books, articles, and web pages, enabling it to generate natural language responses to a wide range of prompts and questions. (This definition was generated by ChatGPT!)

- Can you provide insight into your company's financial performance, including revenue growth, profitability, and cash flow?

- Can you provide details on your company's technology and intellectual property, including any proprietary systems or processes?

- Can you provide insight into your company's culture, including employee morale and satisfaction?

- How do you plan to grow the business in the future, including any plans for expanding into new markets or offering new services?

- Can you discuss any significant risks or uncertainties that may impact the future success of the company?

The best approach to answering any questions you get from buyers is to combine honesty with a positive spin.

Here are some examples:

Q: *Do you want to keep working here after you sell?*

This question expresses concern that if you leave, the enterprise value of the business will decline. If indeed your plan is to leave as soon as you're legally allowed, you need to let the buyer know that this is a possibility, while simultaneously assuaging his worry.

A: I want the company to be as successful as possible, both because of my financial stake in the business and for the sake of my legacy. I've spent the last year grooming my COO to take over as CEO and she is already running more than 75% of the core functions of the business. So I actually think the business will do even better if I move out of the way in the next 12-18 months. I'm willing to stay longer, but my bet is that a few months after you buy us, you'll be convinced that the right decision is for me to cede more responsibility to our COO.

Q: *Why do clients leave you?*

The concern here is that the company is losing too many clients. Given that every agency loses clients on a regular basis, this question will come up during most due diligence discussions.

A: We look at client attrition from two angles: preventable and unpreventable. Preventable attrition means that our team did something wrong that led to the client leaving; unpreventable means it was out of our control, like the client went bankrupt or a new CEO demanded that all agencies be replaced. So we focus on preventable attrition. In the last year, you can see that our preventable attrition dropped every quarter—from 6% of clients in Q1 to 2% of clients in Q4. This happened because the VP of client service started a program at the start of the year where he makes a point of checking in with every client at least once every six weeks. As a result, he was able to identify problems early and course-correct before the client terminated the relationship.

Another important point to remember about management presentations is that they're two-way streets. As such, you should come prepared to ask questions of every buyer as well. After all, you don't want to just sell to the highest offer, you want to sell to someone you're prepared to spend years working alongside. Moreover, like a good job interviewer, asking smart questions of the buyers shows that you're taking the process seriously, and that you're genuinely interested in potentially partnering with them.

Potential questions you could ask might include:

- What makes an acquisition successful and what makes it fail? Can you give examples of prior acquisitions that worked well and others that did not?

- What's your thesis for buying our agency?

- How would you describe your company core values?

- What value add can you provide to us?

WHO ARE THESE PEOPLE IN SUITS?

Management presentations are typically held outside of your business office. Often, this will be your investment banker's office or a hotel meeting room. This is an important detail for one simple reason: Your employees will start to get suspicious if they see lots of people in suits walking in and out of meetings with the executive staff.

Best practice when selling your business is to tell as few people as possible, be very clear with them that no one (even their spouse) should know about the process, and hold meetings offsite.

This is bad for a few reasons. It's a distraction for employees, and it can cause rumors to spread among competitors and clients. The last thing you want is for a competitor to pitch a client by noting, "I heard they're selling and are totally unfocused on running the business right now. Who knows what sort of service you'll get from them after they get absorbed by a giant company!"

The best practice when selling your business is to tell as few people as possible, be very clear with them that no one (even their spouse) should know about the process, and hold meetings offsite.

For the people on your team who are notified that the sale is taking place, an easy way to emphasize the need for strict confidentiality is to say, "Tell nothing, to no one, ever."

At the end of the day, however, it's hard not to raise suspicions about a potential sale. Even if you hold meetings offsite, it's inevitable that the executive team will be gone from the office for numerous days. This in itself raises questions. With this in mind, when I sold my business, I would occasionally say something like this at our company all hands meeting:

"You may see people in suits coming into the office to meet with the executive team. We are a fast growing agency with an amazing reputation. As a result, there are always people who want to invest in us or want us to buy their agency. We're always happy to meet with these folks and consider whatever opportunity is put in front of us. That said, you can be sure that if we ever do decide to do a deal with another company, it will be because it satisfies these three criteria: It's good for employees, it's good for clients, and it's good for the business."

GETTING LETTERS OF INTENT (LOIs)

After all the management meetings are complete (and recall that they should all take place in a period of a week or less), the investment banker sets a due date for letters of intent (LOIs). (In deals that involve many bidders, the process may start with Indications of Intent (IOIs) before moving to LOIs.) An LOI is a non-binding offer for your business. The LOI typically includes the following information—all of which can and should be negotiated by you and your team:

- **The Financial Offer.** How much cash is being paid upfront, and how much will be paid through an earnout? How will the earnout be structured? Will there be a rollover of equity? What payments are guaranteed, and what payments are performance-based? If private equity, will there be an annual management fee paid to the PE firm? Are these fees static or can they be increased over time?

- **Board Makeup.** Will there be a board of directors? How many board seats will you get versus the buyers? How many independent board members will there be, and who gets to nominate and approve them?

- **Future Management Structure**. Will the agency be absorbed into the acquirer? If so, is there a timeline set for this? Will any current management team members be asked to resign? Will the agency retain control of HR, finance, and client services, or will some or all of these be managed by the acquiring firm?

- **Source of Funds**. Where is the buyer getting the cash needed to purchase the agency? Is the cash already "in hand," or does the deal need to be approved by a third party (like a bank or co-investor) before the deal can be consummated? From a seller perspective, the ideal state is that the buyer has cash on-hand without any additional approvals.

- **Required Approvals**. Does the buyer need approvals from financial sources, regulatory agencies, or shareholders prior to finalizing the purchase? Ideally, the buyer should be able to complete the transaction without any of these.

- **Financial or Legal Escrows.** What sort of escrows (reserve accounts) will the buyer require the seller to maintain, how much money will be withheld, and when and how can the seller close the escrows and get her money?

- **Stock**. Will the sellers get the same stock as the buyers? Will there be preferred and common stock or just common stock? Will there be a stock option plan for the sellers and the team? When and how can the buyers buy out the seller's stock (and at what price)?

- **Exclusivity**. Typically, the buyer will ask the seller to agree to a "**no shop**" exclusivity clause. This means that if the seller signs the LOI, he agrees not to negotiate with any other suitors for a period of time while the buyer completes his due diligence and submits a contract to the seller. A typical exclusivity clause lasts no more than 60-90 days, and can be renewed upon expiration if mutually agreed to by both parties. Note: You should strive for the shortest LOI possible (60 days or less) and require milestone check-ins along the way. For example, by day 30, the buyer must acknowledge that all confirmatory due diligence is complete or else the exclusivity period is over. This reduces the buyer's ability to drag out negotiations and use delays to negotiate better terms.

WHY POWER SHIFTS FROM SELLER TO BUYER AFTER THE LOI IS SIGNED

LOIs are always non-binding, which means that neither the buyer nor the seller has any legal obligation to live up to any of the promises made in the document. So, yes, it's possible that a buyer might offer $100 million to a company during the LOI stage and later decide to reduce that offer to $10 million, without any justification at all!

At the same time, deviating from the LOI (without a good reason) is a sign of bad faith, and can result in the other side pulling out of the deal entirely. As a result, buyers who want to get a deal done know that they need to follow through on the terms they put in the LOI.

Buyers also know that the seller is likely getting LOIs from numerous other suitors (and, even if the seller isn't, the investment banker wants the buyers to think that). This drives buyers to make strong initial offers and refrain from too much pushback on seller edits to the LOI terms.

Once the seller signs an LOI with a buyer
and agrees to a period of exclusivity, the
power starts to shift toward the buyer.

Once the seller signs an LOI with a buyer and agrees to a period of exclusivity, the power starts to shift toward the buyer. Why? Because once the seller enters into exclusivity with a buyer, the investment banker tells all of the other bidders that their offers weren't accepted. If the deal with the chosen buyer then falls apart, the investment banker has to go back to all of the other bidders and ask them to consider re-entering the process. Many buyers will then assume that the deal didn't close because of a problem discovered by the winning bidder. As a result, many potential buyers might drop out of the process outright or will only offer a fraction of what they had previously offered.

Therefore, buyers are most highly motivated when they're competing to have their LOI chosen. Sellers are most highly motivated after a winning LOI is signed. Knowing this dynamic, you should negotiate aggressively *prior* to choosing a winning bid and signing that bidder's LOI. The LOI negotiation period is one of the greatest times for a seller to get favorable terms from buyers. First and foremost, this means potentially getting the buyer to raise its offer. It's not uncommon for your investment banker to play two or more buyers off of each other, and to get several improvements in the offer from each (though, at some point, buyers will start to get frustrated and will give you one last and final offer).

The financial terms, however, aren't the only thing you should negotiate during the LOI stage. Strive for a long, highly detailed LOI that clearly articulates the agreement between the parties. Remember, after you sign an LOI and go exclusive with one buyer, your leverage declines. So spending a lot of cycles negotiating a detailed and comprehensive LOI is worth the time and legal fees.

Here's an example of a detailed, seller-favorable term that you might want to add into an LOI. The first time we sold 3Q Digital, the buyer offered us $65 million: $30 million up front in cash, and $35 million based on a three-year performance-based earnout. The LOI, however, did not provide any detail about the mechanics of the earnout. For example, after the deal closed, would we be able to continue managing our client services and sales teams, or would these teams be absorbed into the parent company? Would finances be retained by 3Q, or would revenue and expenses be commingled with the acquirer? Without control, either through mismanagement or financial tricks, we might miss out on some or all of our earnout.

We insisted on a clause in the LOI that made it clear that we would retain control of the business until after the earnout was paid out. It read:

> "Timing for full integration would be no later than the end of the Earnout period, or as early as 3Q Digital would like it to be. Integration prior to the end of the Earnout period (other than as otherwise provided herein) would require the consent of the 3Q Digital Managers and, if appropriate, adjustments to the Earnout criteria to account for any impact that such integration may have on the achievement of the Earnout in full."

In another deal in which I was involved, I insisted that the LOI clearly state that the founders would receive preferred shares in the buyer's company post-merger. This was important because the preferred shares got a guaranteed annual return (a **payment in kind** or **PIK**), which was paid out before common shares, and had substantially better legal rights than the common shares.

After the LOI was signed, the acquirer tried—four times!—to move the founders from preferred shareholders to common shareholders (more on why this is important later). In each case, I referred back to the LOI and asked: "Are you deviating from the LOI because you're acting in bad faith, or because you've forgotten what it said?" After some grumbles from the lawyers, the attempts to give the founders common shares stopped.

CHOOSING A WINNER

Now comes the fun part: choosing a winner. At this point in the process, you've met with numerous potential buyers, gotten several initial offers, and used your investment bank to maximize the financial value and legal rights in these offers.

If you were selling a used car, this part of the process would be straight-forward: The buyer who offered you the most money would be the winner. When selling a business, however, selecting a buyer needs to be more nuanced, looking beyond the headline financial numbers. Here are six factors to consider when choosing the winning buyer (you can weight these as you see fit):

CULTURAL FIT

Once you accept a big check from a buyer, you're signing up to partner with this person or company. In most cases, you'll be expected to commit to a minimum of two years of post-sale involvement in the business. As a result, if the buyer you choose is a jerk, you've just signed up for two years of misery!

In the sales process, the amount of time you spend with each potential buyer is limited. It may consist of an initial phone call, an in-person meeting, or an informal dinner and a few follow up calls. Remember that everyone vying for your business is going to be on their best behavior. These two factors make it difficult to assess whether a potential buyer is going to be difficult to work with once the deal closes.

There are a few ways to mitigate this. First, look for subtle examples of bad behavior. For example, perhaps the buyer tells you one thing verbally and then includes a contradictory clause in the LOI. Or maybe the buyer does the classic "kiss up, kick down" maneuver—they're nice to you, but obnoxious to the junior people on their team.

You can (and should) call references. Are the references recent (good) or ancient (bad)? Are they glowing reviews or lukewarm?

Backchanneling is also a good strategy. Use LinkedIn to find people you know who are connected to the buyers or, better still, were acquired by them. Be careful not to reveal too much about your process. Tell the contact, for example, that you were introduced to the company in question by a mutual acquaintance and you were just doing some background research on them.

In one of my deals, I got a very strong financial offer from a large agency. I really liked the CEO, and I thought there would be great synergy between our two companies. I was about to sign an LOI with the buyer, when I decided to backchannel with a friend of mine who had sold his agency to them a few years earlier. In the conversation, he explained to me that this company only cared about revenue and cut out all employee training because it wasn't revenue producing. This one call alone led me to back away from the deal.

VISION AND VALUE ADD

Not all buyers are created equal. Some buyers are highly strategic and bring a well-honed playbook of ideas that have been proven to increase value in their investments. Others are mainly focused on financial optimization. By cutting costs, raising prices, and using debt financing, they assume they can quickly increase the value of the agency and sell it for a profit.

To be clear, it's rare that an investor will openly admit: "We just cut costs and raise prices, and flip you as fast as possible." Almost every potential buyer will claim that they have a bevy of secret strategies to improve your business. The reality, however, is that many investors don't provide much strategy to their acquisitions.

The easiest way to understand whether an investor is going to bring strategic value is to do two things. First, ask to see their playbook. What tactics have they used again and again to increase the value of their acquisitions (beyond just cutting costs and raising prices)? Second, check references and specifically ask companies in the buyer's portfolio how the buyer added value.

GOAL ALIGNMENT

Some founders want to remain CEO of their agency for years after they sell. Others want to exit entirely as soon as the transaction is complete. Some founders want almost all their cash compensation up front. Others want to roll the dice and make a lot of the compensation contingent on their future performance.

Whatever your personal and financial objectives, some deals will squarely align with your goals and others won't. Choose an offer that matches your goals.

LIKELIHOOD OF CLOSING

Some buyers have a reputation of winning LOIs, but rarely closing their deals. As noted previously, this is bad for you as a seller, because a deal that falls apart after an LOI is signed is often perceived as a signal by other buyers that something bad was discovered during due diligence by the winning bidder. As a result, these buyers may decline to bid on your business the second time around, or significantly reduce their offer terms.

Doing due diligence may help you avoid these buyers. Ideally, your investment banker should have enough experience in the agency M&A space to know which buyers present the highest risk of an aborted deal.

GUARANTEED CASH

On average, most deals provide sellers with between 45% and 75% of the deal value in cash up front and the remainder as an earnout or rollover. For some sellers, getting as much cash up front is the priority. This may be because the dollar amounts are large enough to give them financial security for life, or it may be that they assume that any **contingent payments** could be worthless, so it's better to maximize guaranteed money. Whatever the reason, some sellers would rather accept a lower overall offer in exchange for more guaranteed money.

TOTAL COMPENSATION

The total return on a deal is the combination of upfront guaranteed cash plus the earnout or rollover. Many buyers will argue that the non-guaranteed (also known as "contingent") portion will be worth many times the initial cash.

In many cases, they're correct. When an M&A deal goes well, company profit increases (good for earnouts), and the value of the acquired company increases (good for rollovers).

Consider this scenario: A company is acquired for $100 million: $60 million in cash up front, and $40 million in rollover equity (representing 40% of the new company's total equity). Three years later, the company sells for $300 million. The 40% rollover is now worth $120 million, creating a total return for the sellers of $180 million.

Of course, not all deals are successful. The contingent payments may end up being worth nothing if the company's performance stalls. And some buyers purposely throw out large contingency payment amounts that they know will be impossible for the seller to obtain. For example, a buyer may offer a seller $150 million with $60 million in cash up front and up to $90 million of contingent payments. To get the entire $90 million, however, the seller needs to triple its EBITDA in 18 months. In reality, the buyer (and, hopefully, the seller) realize that a realistic outcome is roughly 50% of the target, resulting in $45 million of likely contingent payment for a total compensation of $105 million. Thus, when considering the total compensation of an offer, try not to be blinded by the headline numbers. Instead, take a realistic view of your future performance, and use that as your guide.

WHAT IF THERE ISN'T A WINNER?

In *Hoop Dreams*, an amazing documentary about two inner city high school basketball stars, William Gates—one of the high schoolers—says, "When somebody say, 'When you get to the NBA, don't forget about me,' and that stuff. Well, I should have said to them, 'If I don't make it, don't you forget about me.'"[4]

No matter how amazing your agency is, or how many prospective buyers tell you they plan to submit a way-above-market offer, your sale may never happen. You might suffer a major client loss that

---

[4] https://www.imdb.com/title/tt0110057/characters/nm0309637.

scares away potential buyers, the economy might collapse, or the offers you get just might not be good enough for you to want to accept them. You may also get an amazing offer, sign an LOI, and then see the deal fall apart during due diligence.

For this reason, it's vital that you continue to manage your business under the assumption that your sale isn't going to happen. In other words, make decisions—both day-to-day management and future planning—as if you're not considering a potential sale. If you start to either get distracted by the sales process or make decisions based on what you think potential buyers want, you run the risk of putting all of your eggs in the "sell the business" basket. If the deal falls apart, you're stuck with a business that's been ignored for months or with investments that you wouldn't have otherwise made.

Tell your executive staff (the few folks who know about the potential sale) that it's business as usual at the company. Let these leaders know that they should assume that a deal will never happen. And act this way yourself.

With that said, it may be advisable to put off making aggressive, potentially disruptive decisions until after the deal closes—if you can do this without negatively impacting the business. For example, if you're thinking about firing one or more of your C-level executives, doing so during a process or due diligence may spook potential buyers. If waiting a few months won't destroy the business, hold off!

In general, however, don't put the business on hold during a process—operate on the assumption that you won't "make it to the NBA" and need to wake up tomorrow and run the agency.

- Selling an agency involves a series of orchestrated steps and documentation. The first is to get your business data in order, which means having your finances prepared using GAAP, creating a Quality of Earnings (QofE) report, and creating a teaser and confidential information memorandum (CIM) that highlights the strengths of your business (financial performance, clients, proprietary tech, leadership team, competitive advantages, future strategy).

- Investment bankers will use this information to reach out to prospective buyers. Interested and qualified buyers will be invited to meet with the agency leadership team in management meetings. They'll then submit letters of intent (LOIs) with details of their proposed offer to buy the agency.

- The investment bank and agency will weigh the different LOIs and potentially play different buyers off each other, in an attempt to get better terms and financial value in the LOI. The agency should choose a winner based in part on the best offer it receives, but also on whether the acquirer would be a good cultural fit and provide value add to help grow the agency in the future.

- Continue to operate the agency as if no deal will ever get signed.

CHAPTER SEVEN

NEGOTIATING THE DEAL

The father of a high school friend of mine wrote several books in the 1980s that became massively popular Hollywood action movies. When he sold the rights to the movies to a Hollywood studio, he was given a "points deal," meaning that he got a percentage of the profits from each movie.

The movies were blockbusters (anyone aged 13 or older in the 1980s saw at least one of them). And yet, when it came time for my friend's father to get paid, he got nothing. The studios, it turns out, were very good at making profit, but also at moving money around so that an individual movie looked like it was just breaking even.

I don't know if this story is real (it's legend in my hometown), but it serves an important point: Whatever deal you think you've negotiated is only as good as the deal you actually sign. Having a great legal team, paying attention to details, and getting everything in writing is crucial to getting a deal done that gets you what you deserve.

HIRING A GREAT LAW FIRM

In the 13 years that I ran 3Q, I worked with seven law firms. Some of these were one-person solo shops. Others were 1000+ lawyer multinational giants. In two of the deals I signed, I fired one law firm mid-process and replaced them with another. In both cases, these decisions likely resulted in millions of dollars of additional value for me and my management team.

WHEN SHOULD YOU HIRE A LAW FIRM?

It's never too early to interview law firms. There are many reasons why a law firm would decline to work with you, and you need to eliminate these firms long before you have an urgent need for legal help. Some firms only work with very large clients. Others have M&A groups that specialize in certain types of deals (technology acquisitions, for example). Depending upon who may be acquiring you, some firms may be "conflicted out," because they already do work for your acquirer. And some firms may be booked solid with work at the time that you need them and cannot take on your business.

For all of these reasons, you should have a roster of at least two or three firms that you like, have experience selling agencies or service businesses, want to work with you, and are unlikely to have a conflict.

You don't need to retain the firm to do all of your legal work—you can explicitly work with them on just your transaction-related needs. Given that partners at top lawyers may charge over $1000 an hour, it's often overkill for an agency to pay $15,000 for 15 hours of contract review. Find a cheaper lawyer to do that work for you. But, as you near the IOI or LOI stage, you need to have a firm that's ready to work with you.

FACTORS IN HIRING A LAW FIRM

Here are five factors that are important when considering law firms:

- **Do Conflict Checks Early**. The moment you know against whom you will be negotiating, let your potential law firm know, so that they can run a conflict check. In most cases, if you're negotiating against a company larger than yours, the law firm will turn down business from you in order to preserve their relationship with the bigger company (they assume that they'll get repeat business from the larger firm and that this is the only time you will need a lot of legal work).

- **Size Matters**. The bigger the deal, the bigger the law firm you need. There are two reasons for this. First, big law firms have lawyers who specialize in every aspect of business law: employment, tax, corporate, bankruptcy, contracts, real estate, international and, of course, M&A. Big acquisitions are usually pretty complex and will require different experts to join the negotiations as needed. Ideally, you want "one throat to choke"—one law firm that can handle all of your needs. Trying to work with several small firms with different expertise creates transactional costs, mistakes, and delay. And, ultimately, it might not save you any money.

  Second, the size of your law firm sends a signal to the other side that you are a savvy negotiator. When a big law firm realizes they're negotiating against another big law firm, they tend to treat the other side with more respect and are less likely to try to push aggressive terms.

  As with the choice of an investment bank, it's important to make sure that you aren't the smallest or largest client of your law firm. This is particularly important when you're considering a large firm. If the M&A team is working on deals for you, Google, and AT&T, you can be certain that you're not going to be the priority. So while bigger is better, too big is bad when it comes to law firms.

Note that you don't have to work with a firm in your city. Most deals rely on Delaware law, and every corporate lawyer in America knows the ins and outs of Delaware law. As such, if you're in a high-priced area like San Francisco, New York, or LA, you may be able to get top-notch representation for 50% less than the local prices, simply by working with a firm based in a smaller city like Seattle or Denver.

- **Pick the Lawyer, Not the Firm.** Large law firms spend millions of dollars establishing a brand for their firm. The reality, however, is that law firms of a similar size are all basically the same. Some may offer slightly better technology or have an office that's closer to yours, but it's not as if one firm has some secret strategic negotiating book that no one else has.

  As a result, the only thing that really matters is the lawyers who work on your deal. Thus, you need to make it clear to the firm that you're interviewing specific lawyers within their firm, and that when you're ready to move forward, you will only be working with those people. This should include the senior partner and all associates on her team, as a lot of the day-to-day work will be done by associates and junior partners (and paralegals).

  The best M&A lawyers have a few traits. First, they embrace conflict. M&A negotiation is often very tense. Expect your lawyers to get into numerous heated debates with the other side. A lawyer who isn't willing to raise his voice from time to time or walk away from the table isn't well suited for M&A work.

> *Great M&A lawyers use the law strategically. This is a nuanced but very important point. A lot of lawyers know the law well, but don't know how to apply the law to a business situation.*

Second, great M&A lawyers use the law strategically. This is a nuanced but very important point. A lot of lawyers know the law well, but don't know how to apply the law to a business situation. For example, I was once in a dispute with a large, publicly traded partner of 3Q. I asked my law firm whether we should file a suit against the public company. The partner responded: "Why bother, you won't win." I responded: "Do you mean the case will be thrown out immediately by the judge before going to trial, or that if we go to trial, we will lose?" The lawyer indicated that it was the latter outcome that he meant.

I then asked a follow up: if we told the public company that we were about to file a suit, would they be worried that they would have to disclose this suit in their public filings, potentially creating a PR problem for them and decreasing the price of their stock? Would the mere threat of a suit cause them to negotiate with us? The lawyers agreed, we threatened the suit, and we settled. I then fired those lawyers.

I've noticed that many lawyers are afraid, or simply don't know how to apply the law to business outcomes. Often, when asked for strategic guidance, lower quality lawyers will cop out by saying, "That's a business decision." A great lawyer puts herself in your shoes and tries to use the law to protect your rights. This is the type of person you want on your side during M&A negotiations.

I'll note there are many strategic lawyers who've left big firms to either start their own law firm or work at a smaller firm (the pressures and bureaucracy of large firms often spur such a move). These lawyers can hold their own against large firms on the other side of the table, but also charge a lot less than the mega firms. Thus, while I do believe that law firm size matters in M&A, if you can find a former large firm M&A attorney who is working at a smaller firm, this may be a great option. Indeed, after we fired the big law firm described previously for not being strategic enough, we switched to a ten person firm made up of Big Law refugees. That firm made several strategic moves that were crucial to our success in our negotiations.

- **Demand Clarity on Business Terms**. The first time I sold 3Q, I worked with a large, prestigious law firm. The deal took about six months to complete, and the firm provided us with an array of impressive lawyers to help us close the deal. The one thing the firm didn't do too well was provide regular billing updates (not that it's a good excuse, I was so focused on closing the deal that I didn't notice).

  When the deal closed, I got a bill for $550,000—more than twice what I expected the cost to be. I asked the senior partner why the bill was so high and he explained to me that—midway through the negotiations—they had raised their hourly rates for all of their staff (and hadn't bothered to tell me). I ended up getting a $50,000 discount, but I still paid way more than I thought I should.

Make sure you understand everything about your business relationship with a potential law firm:

- How frequently do they bill you (or at least provide you with a billing summary)? It should be weekly and no less than monthly.

- Can they raise the hourly rates without notifying you?

- Do they need your permission to add extra attorneys to a call or a meeting? If left unchecked, some law firms will put six $500 an hour attorneys on a conference call, costing you $3000 for one call!

- In what time increment do they bill in? Lawyers usually bill in six-minute increments.

- What charges will you be paying beyond attorney hours? Often, this might include photocopying, the online **data room**, travel, paralegals, and administrative costs.

- **Do Reference Checks**. Ask the firm to provide you with references from companies like you (or even better, use your network to find colleagues who've worked with the firm to get more unfiltered opinions!).

THE DUE DILIGENCE PROCESS

After the LOI is signed by all parties, the clock on the exclusivity period for the buyer to complete the deal begins. During this time period, the buyer must complete all due diligence and negotiate a signed purchase agreement with the seller. Once the exclusivity period ends, the seller can elect to talk to other suitors.

The point of due diligence is to confirm that the agency for sale is as valuable as the buyer thought it was when he made his offer. Thus, it's OK for the buyer to discover some unexpected negative aspects of the selling agency, as long as the negative surprises don't reduce the value below the offer price (though, as we'll see, even then a deal might get done).

As much as you might sometimes feel offended by some of the questions the buyer is asking, remember they're taking a huge risk by buying your business, and they have an obligation to ask tough questions.

Due diligence can be exhausting. Not just because the buyer will ask for reams of documents and follow up with many, detailed questions, but because it often feels like you're being interrogated by the police in a dark room in the basement of a police station. As noted earlier, buying an agency is a tricky proposition. The buyer is mostly buying people, and people can walk out the door—leaving the buyer with an empty bank account and a dying business.

So as much as you might sometimes feel offended by some of the questions the buyer is asking, remember they're taking a huge risk by buying your business, and they have an obligation to ask tough questions.

At the onset of due diligence, the seller sets up a data room—an online repository in which all relevant documents will be submitted for the seller to evaluate. It's often the case that the buyer will also set up a data room to share relevant documents with the buyer. This is especially the case when there's a large contingent payment as part of the transaction, or if the seller is accepting buyer equity as part of the consideration.

A typical data room might look like this:

- 📁 A. Corporate Documents
- 📁 B. Equityholder Information and Securities
- 📁 C. Contracts
- 📁 D. Litigation
- 📁 E. Real Estate
- 📁 F. Intellectual Property – IP
- 📁 G. Information Technology- IT
- 📁 H. Outstanding Debt Obligations
- 📁 I. Mergers – Acquisitions – Dispositions
- 📁 J. Insurance
- 📁 K. Employee Benefit Plans
- 📁 L. Human Resources
- 📁 M. Financials
- 📁 N. Marketing and Sales
- 📁 Z. Due Diligence Trackers

Source: Garros Group

The buyer then provides the seller with a due diligence plan or schedule, itemizing all the items they want answered. Due diligence requests can broadly be divided into two areas:

- Foundational (also known as Confirmatory) due diligence—making sure that the basic foundations of the company are sound.

- Business opportunity due diligence—verifying that the business is on a good trajectory with a smart strategy and sound leadership.

Here's a sample of the dozens of requests you might expect during typical due diligence:

- Revenue, gross margin, and EBITDA by client for the last few years.

- A list of all clients, with revenue and tenure. Discussion of client attrition and historical attrition data.

- A technology overview, including information about the legal terms and cost of each technology vendor, and a deep dive into any proprietary technology the agency has built.

- Sales pipeline and completed sales over the last few years.

- Staffing overview with salaries and org chart.

- Complete financial results from the last few years. This will often be covered by the Quality of Earnings report.

- Real estate costs and legal obligations.

- Client and vendor references.

Business opportunity due diligence might include:

- A competitive or Strengths/Weaknesses/Opportunities/ Threats (SWOT) analysis of the company versus key competitors.

- Projections on the general health of the industry in which the agency operates.

- The company's vision for the future and what investments will be necessary to achieve that vision.

The net result of all of these questions is, first, a lot of documents will be uploaded to the data room. Most sellers will want to see all contracts with clients, all real estate leases, complete and detailed financials, detailed sales win/loss data and pipeline projections, and comprehensive HR files for the entire organization. Secondly, the sellers will be expected to produce presentations that address all the business opportunity questions. While much of this is duplicative of what was presented in the CIM or management meetings, the buyer will now want to delve much deeper into the company's business opportunities.

As noted, agencies are risky acquisitions, both because the human capital (the staff) may leave, or the revenue (clients) may decline. So expect the due diligence to be comprehensive, turning over every possible stone. Buyers will want to dig deep to make sure that the data shows that you're a stable, profitable, and growing business. Don't be offended by this (up to a point). This is just part of the process!

TELLING MORE PEOPLE—CLIENTS AND STAFF

At this stage, it's often necessary to inform more members of the team that a potential sale is taking place. So, for example, the head of sales may be required to do a deep dive into the sales performance and strategy, and the head of client services may be asked to explain why some clients leave and how the agency grows revenue from existing clients. Remember: the best practice in M&A is to tell as few people as possible that a deal is happening (loose lips sink ships). It's important to only involve more people when it's absolutely necessary. Wait as long as you can to involve them (in the event the deal falls apart before they're needed), and demand absolute confidentiality from them.

Inevitably, a buyer will also want to do reference calls with your top clients. This is also a tricky moment, as an acquisition can be seen as a negative by some clients, in that it creates uncertainty about the future and can disrupt service during the integration of the business into the new owner's operating structure. Ultimately, it's pretty hard to sell an agency without giving the buyer a chance to hear from top clients, especially if these clients make up a large percentage of the agency's revenue and profit.

The best advice in this situation is threefold. First, push to have as few clients as possible do reference calls. Ideally, I would shoot for two or three clients, especially if they're large clients. If your revenue is evenly spread among many clients, a buyer may ask for many references (upwards of 15). Buyers may also ask to speak to clients that have left the agency. Here the objective is to find clients that left on a good note!

Second, try to have the client reference calls process be done later in the overall M&A process (after almost every other due diligence issue has been resolved), and certainly after a first draft of the purchase agreement has been received, and seems to be on track.

Lastly, when you ask the client to be a reference, use it as a selling opportunity to get them excited about the potential deal. The call (not an email, which would be too impersonal) might sound something like this:

> "Bob, first, I want to thank you and your team for your partnership over the last five years. We're really proud to have helped you grow and we love working with everyone over there. I have some exciting news that I want to share, as well as a favor I need from you. The news is that we're likely going to be acquired by XYZ Agency. We've been approached by a lot of agencies looking to join forces with us. We chose XYZ because we think they're really going to help us provide even better results to clients like you. Not only do they share our cultural values and unwavering commitment to client success, they also happen to have more than 500 people in Asia, which I know will help you as you look to expand

internationally. They also have an award-winning out-of-home media buying team, which could really complement the metro-targeted campaigns we're running digitally at the moment.

I really think this is going to be a big win for both of our companies. Here's the ask.

XYZ agency wants to talk to our top clients as part of their due diligence process. I don't think this would be more than a 30-minute call and you wouldn't have to reveal anything that you feel is confidential. It's really just to make sure that our relationship is solid, and that the work we're doing for you is as great as we've told them.

Would it be OK if I introduced you to Jenny at XYZ?"

BAD NEWS AND RETRADES

Inevitably, when you send over hundreds of pages of documents, present hours of strategy, have accountants scrutinize your financials, and ask clients and vendors to share references about your business, something unexpected and negative is going to show up about your agency. No business is perfect. Clients leave, employees quit, financial goals are missed, competitors win a big account, and so on—all of this happens to even the best agencies.

The second time we sold 3Q, we signed the non-binding LOI in the last week of December. As we started the due diligence process in January, we found out that two of our larger clients were terminating their contracts with us. One was leaving because they had hired a new CMO (a change in management is the number one reason an agency loses a client). The other left because we had done such a good job of growing their marketing programs that they felt it was now such a crucial part of the business that they had to hire an entire in-house team to manage it. Neither of these really reflected badly on our agency and our potential, but it did take a big bite out of our EBITDA performance.

The investors, however, were spooked. They worried that they were buying a company that was now worth 10% less than when they signed the LOI a month prior. Ultimately, this left them with three choices: drop out of the deal, wait and see if our numbers improved, or ask for a reduction in price. In our case, the investors opted to wait and see if we rebounded, which we did. After a few months of strong sales growth, our EBITDA was back up to where it had been when we signed the deal, assuaging the investors' concerns.

In many cases, however, buyers actively look for reasons to reduce the price they agreed to pay for your business in the LOI. This is known as a "retrade." Any misstep by the seller is an excuse for these types of buyers to discount the price. You missed your monthly target? Retrade! You lost a client? Retrade! A senior team member quit? Retrade! You got eliminated from an Request for Proposal (RFP)? Retrade!

This sometimes reminds me of the "Heads I win, tails you lose" game that some clients like to play. When a campaign is exceeding performance, the client is happy and pays his bill in full (but offers no bonuses for exceptional performance). When a campaign is underperforming, the client asks for a discount. In the M&A world, there are buyers who quickly demand a discount when your business underperforms, but refuse to pay more when the business exceeds expectations.

Ultimately, it's up to you to decide if requests for retrades are fair (which they sometimes are, if there's a material decline in the business), or if they're borderline unethical attempts to pay less than what the buyer had just agreed. As noted, bad news happens to even the greatest agencies. A buyer expecting to get a discount for every negative incident is probably not a good long-term partner.

KEY TAKEAWAYS FROM THIS CHAPTER

- Hiring a great lawyer is as important as finding the right investment banker. While it's preferable to work with a reputable firm who the opposing side will respect, finding a great lawyer who has experience in M&A negotiating and will think like a CEO is key to having a successful outcome.

- The buyer will submit a lengthy due diligence request list, which includes detailed information about financials, an org chart, client contracts, sales pipeline, and client references. As the amount and level of detail in these requests increases, it will likely be necessary to tell select staff and clients about the potential deal. This should be done thoughtfully and with as few people as possible.

- Be careful of "retrades," where buyers attempt to use findings in due diligence to reduce the offer detailed in the LOI. While a reduction in value is sometimes justified, this is sometimes a borderline unethical tactic designed to create extra value for the buyer.

CHAPTER EIGHT

GETTING THE
CONTRACT RIGHT

The first time I sold 3Q, I was selling to a public company with a relatively new CEO. The CEO was a friendly, dynamic, fast-moving leader who had been brought in to turn around the buyer quickly. Toward the end of the contract negotiations, there was a particularly sticky clause that I just couldn't accept. I had a good rapport with the CEO so I called him to discuss it. He listened to my concern and replied: "David, trust me, I'll make sure that we treat you right after the deal closes." To which I replied: "As my Rabbi once told me, 'Trust in Allah but watch your camels.' I trust you, but if you get hit by a bus tomorrow, I may not trust the new CEO, so I need everything in writing."

The CEO understood, and he made sure that the clause I was concerned about was corrected. We signed the deal and six months later, the CEO was fired.

In this section, we'll talk about how to negotiate a contract and key clauses that deserve your focus.

HOW TO NEGOTIATE

Here are a few tips on how to negotiate the best deal for your business:

- **The Four Corners of the Document**. One thing I learned in law school is that it's important to get everything in writing. Whatever was described in the LOI, mentioned in an email, or discussed over the phone is largely irrelevant if it isn't included in the "four corners of the document." This is a term lawyers use to describe what's in the contract—anything discussed that's not written down on paper has substantially less legal weight. Make sure that every deal point is clearly and explicitly included in the purchase agreement. Another legal expression to know is "that which is not included is implicitly excluded."

- **Play Good Cop, Bad Cop**. Few contract negotiations involving millions of dollars changing hands don't have moments of tension and frustration. As a seller, you want to avoid too much confrontation with the buyer, if for no other reason than you'll be working with them for many years to come. This is why it's common for your attorneys (and to a degree, your investment banker) to take the role of the "bad cop" in negotiations while you play the "good cop." You can be tough as nails behind the scenes, but playing a little dumb during negotiations and deferring to the lawyers is often advisable.

- **Never Split the Difference.** If you haven't read the book, *Never Split the Difference* by former FBI hostage negotiator Christopher Voss, go read it! As the title implies, rookie negotiators often think that splitting the difference is a sign of success. In many cases, however, they're up against savvy foes who start with an extreme position to make it seem like the middle is a reasonable compromise when in fact it's just slightly less extreme.[1]

- **Beware the Eleventh Hour Ask**. A friend of mine who sold his business to professional investors gave me this advice. This is a tactic where the opposing side demands a change or addition to the contract after you thought negotiations were complete. It puts you in a difficult position—you thought you were moments away from signing the deal, and now you have to decide whether to devalue the deal by accepting a new term or potentially losing the deal if you reject the change. In most cases, this is an aggressive bluff—the other side wants to close the deal as much as you do, and they're just trying to get a little more value from you. Don't be afraid to say no!

- **Know Your BATNA**. BATNA stands for the "Best Alternative to a Negotiated Agreement." In other words, what are your options if you decide to walk away from the deal? As noted, deal negotiations are often stressful and confrontational. Someone once told me "a successful deal means that both parties are somewhat unhappy about the outcome." So it's unlikely that you're going to go through the entire negotiation without a few moments of anger, disappointment, and hesitation about moving forward.

  You may, however, get to a point where the deal no longer makes sense, or where you have insurmountable trust issues with the other side. In that situation, consider alternative outcomes. If your agency is thriving, or if you were already on

---

[1]Chris Voss and Tahl Raz, *Never Split the Difference: Negotiating As If Your Life Depended On It*, (New York: Harper, 2016).

the fence about whether you really wanted to sell or not, you have a strong BATNA. Simply call the buyer and tell them you've decided not to sell at this time. In many cases, this will cause the buyer to back down from aggressive positions and try to get you back to the table.

Another option may be to let the exclusivity period expire and then renew conversations with other bidders. Or, you may want to consider some of the alternatives to selling discussed earlier (taking debt financing, becoming chairman of the board, etc.).

The main point is that there are always alternatives to continuing to negotiate a deal about which you have doubts. It's good to internalize these options before you start your negotiation.

If you've spent $500,000 on a sales process and you end up faced with a contract that you don't think is good for the business, you shouldn't sign it. Period.

- **Say No to Sunk Costs; Say Yes to Pot Odds.** As soon as you start the sales process, you start to incur costs and invest time in a potential sale. And every step in the process just gets more expensive and takes up more time. There's a natural human tendency to worry about "sunk costs" and conclude that a deal must get done to recoup these costs. But there are two important things to know about sunk costs.

  First, you shouldn't factor them into your decision as to whether or not to move forward with a potential sale. If you've spent $500,000 on a sales process and you end up faced with a contract that you don't think is good for the business, you shouldn't sign it. Period. A good analogy here comes from the world of poker. In the game "Hold 'Em," there are four rounds of betting. As each round progresses, a player's chances of winning changes (depending on the cards revealed in each round). A player may have a high percentage chance of winning after the first three rounds of betting, but by the last bet, they'll see the likelihood of victory plummet if the cards don't go their way.

When faced with a large bet from another player during the last round, an inexperienced player may think, "I have a very low chance of winning, but I've already invested this much into the game, I have to call the bet." A seasoned player, however, disregards sunk costs and thinks about "pot odds." Pot odds is simply the percentage chance of winning versus the percentage of the overall pot that the player needs to bet to stay in the game.

Let's say that Player A has invested $500 into a hand over the first three rounds of betting, and she gets to the last round. Player B bets $1000, which raises the total pot to $5,000. Player A estimates that she has a 10% chance of winning the pot. Because a $1000 bet would result in investing 20% of the pot, the pot odds suggest that Player A should fold. Even though it hurts to fold after having invested $500 to get to the final round, Player A concludes that it will hurt a lot less to lose $500 than to lose $1500.

Thus, when thinking about whether to move forward with a deal, don't factor in how much you've spent working with a potential acquirer. Focus exclusively on whether the deal is a good one for your business.

The second point is that many buyers fall prey to sunk cost thinking. It's often the case that there's an internal sponsor or champion at the buyer who has been advocating to buy your agency. This champion has put their reputation—and potentially their job—on the line and is under a lot of pressure to get the deal done.

As the buyer's time and cost commitments increase, the internal champion's sunk cost pressure increases in lock step. If you're negotiating from a pot odds perspective and the buyer has sunk cost pressure, you have leverage! You may be comfortable walking away, which may drive the buyer to make concessions to avoid losing the deal.

COMMON DOCUMENTS

The average business contract (like the ones you sign with your clients) is around five to ten pages long and has one signature from your agency and one from the other party. Not only are acquisition documents longer, there are often many separate documents that need to be negotiated, and multiple parties must sign them. Generally, there are four documents to which you need to pay the closest attention:

- **The Merger or Acquisition Agreement**. Also known as the **Security Purchase Agreement (SPA),** this spells out the rights and obligations of each party at the moment of contract signature. It covers such issues as the purchase price, indemnification, and representations and warranties.

- **The Articles of Incorporation**. This document outlines how the company will be run once the deal is completed. It includes how the board will be elected and managed, what happens when the company is sold or raises money, the rights of shareholders, and the form and location of incorporation. This contract normally only applies to deals where either the seller is remaining a stand-alone company or the buyer and seller are merging to create an entirely new company. With Hold Co deals or PE add-on deals, the seller is simply absorbed into the existing company, so no new articles of incorporation are required.

- **Your Employment Contract.** The key employees of the acquired agency will usually be expected to sign employment contracts that spell out their duties, compensation, and legal responsibilities. Importantly, this document also defines the rights of an employee who is terminated.

- **The Waterfall and Flow of Funds.** The **waterfall** is usually an Excel document that shows who owns what percentage of the company after the deal closes, and the type of shares that they own. If there's a distribution of money, the waterfall determines the **flow of funds**—who gets paid, in what order, and how much. It's important to scrutinize this document carefully to make sure that a lazy lawyer didn't mess up the math on payments. Later in this chapter, I'll share an example of how a basic math mistake had millions of dollars of impact.

The total number of documents you will sign will be more than these four—the last deal I did required signatures on 15 documents, with the longest being 72 pages!

KEY TERMS TO NEGOTIATE

A typical acquisition includes hundreds of clauses across many pages and documents, so we can't discuss every last term that might come up. Please note that I am not a licensed attorney, so do not take any of my commentary as legal advice! That said, there are certain terms in an acquisition that are crucial to understand and negotiate very carefully.

BOARD OF DIRECTORS

The board of directors runs a corporation. They almost always have the power to fire the CEO, raise money, sell the company, approve or deny investment requests, and even set strategy. As a result, it's crucial to create a board that's made up of people you trust and respect, and to ensure that the rules that govern board behavior are fair.

Note that it's rare for an acquired company to get board seats if you're being purchased by a publicly traded company, such as a holding company, or by a company much larger than you. Board seats are more important with acquisitions by companies near your size, or when a private equity company buys your company and creates a new corporation to run the business moving forward. As a ballpark number, if you own at least 10% of the company moving forward, you should have at least one board seat and some control over how the board operates.

With that in mind, here are key points to negotiate with respect to the board:

- **Board Appointments and Additions**. How are board members appointed, and can the number of board members be increased or decreased? Because the board controls the company, any change in board makeup can have a major impact on the fate of your business.

  For example, let's say that you control three board seats and your investor controls four, and your articles of incorporation state that any "change of control" (e.g., sale) decision must be made by at least five board members (thus allowing you veto power). If, however, the addition and approval of new board members can be made with a simple majority, your investors could add another seat to the board and place someone in that seat who votes in-line with them. With that additional seat, they would now have the requisite five board seats to vote for a change of control, regardless of your vote.

- **Board Meetings**. Can board meetings be held without you? In some contracts, no notice of a board meeting is necessary if a majority of the board is present. During that meeting, the board may be able to vote on crucial issues. Because you will likely control a minority of the board votes, this could mean that your buyer could hold a meeting without notifying you.

  In instances where you're being bought by a much larger company and no board seat will be made available to you, you may be able to ask for **board observer** status and/or **information rights**. A board observer is invited to attend the meeting, but does not have a vote. Information rights give you access to financial results and board decks. Both of these rights are good ways to monitor board behavior and ensure that nothing nefarious is taking place.

- **Board Votes**. What types of votes require unanimous votes, and which require a simple majority? Do board votes require a minimum notification period? Do you need to be present to vote, or can you vote remotely? As the minority on the board, you want as many votes as possible to require at least one of your board votes to pass.

COSTS AND PAYMENTS

Have you ever booked a hotel with a nightly rate of $199, only to receive a bill for $285 and discover that the quoted rate didn't include tax, "resort fees," and other hidden costs? Hidden fees can rear their ugly head during M&A as well, except that in this case, it could cost you millions.

- **Closing Costs. Closing costs** are expenses paid by the buyer and seller to outside parties during a transaction. Typically, this includes lawyers, accountants, consultants, investment bankers, and travel. Some buyers, however, may attempt to recoup the cost of having their own teams work on the deal. This is a potential area of dispute and can be very costly if you agree to pay it. The best practice is to spell out what is and isn't included in closing costs in the LOI and to set a cap on how much can be recovered if it's to be included in the closing costs.

  Typically, costs on both sides aren't reimbursed, but rather result in an addition or deduction of the final deal value. For example, let's say that the total deal value is $20 million, and the buyer claims $2 million of closing costs from lawyers and accountants, and the seller claims $1 million. The deal value would be adjusted to $19 million.

- **Escrow**. Escrow is a portion of the deal proceeds kept in reserve for a defined period of time. This money is intended to compensate the buyer for unforeseen costs that the seller should have covered. A common example is a tax escrow. If the IRS audits the seller's company and determines that the seller owes back taxes that occurred prior to the acquisition by the buyer, the buyer can use the tax escrow to cover the additional tax bill they must now pay.

  In general, you can negotiate three things about escrow: how long the escrow lasts, how much is in escrow, and how and when the escrow can be accessed by the buyer. Generally, sellers want the smallest escrow for the shortest time with the most restrictive rules around buyers getting the funds. Your lawyers and investment banker should be able to advise you on whether the escrow terms requested by the buyer are reasonable.

- **Management Fees**. It's common for private equity investors to ask for an annual management fee from the company they're buying. This fee may be a flat fee, or it may be variable (as a percentage of annual EBITDA, for example). The good news is that this fee can be excluded from EBITDA (thereby increasing the adjusted EBITDA) in a future sale. The bad news is that the fee can get quite large, especially if it varies with the company's EBITDA.

  From the seller perspective, the goal is to define this fee in the LOI as clearly as possible, and to preferably make it very low and not increasable as EBITDA increases. After all, if you as the founder own 20% of the company and your private equity firm is taking 5% of $10 million of EBITDA ($500K), 20% of that—$100,000—is your money!

- **Net Working Capital (NWC) and Cash-Free, Debt Free (CF/DF)**. **Cash-free, debt-free (CFDF)** and **net working capital** are both important financial metrics used to evaluate a company's financial health and stability.

  Net working capital is a measure of a company's short-term financial health and is calculated as the difference between its current assets and current liabilities. It represents the resources available to a company to fund its daily operations.

  Current assets are assets that can be converted into cash within one year, such as cash, accounts receivable, and inventory. Current liabilities are debts that must be paid within one year, such as accounts payable, short-term loans, and taxes owed.

  A company with a positive net working capital is considered to have sufficient liquidity to meet its short-term obligations, while negative net working capital may indicate that the company is facing financial difficulties and may not be able to pay its debts as they come due.

When a company is sold on a CF/DF basis, the buyer and seller agree that neither the cash currently in the company nor the debts that the company currently owes will be included in the purchase price.

Where CF/DF and NWC collide is during the determination of how much NWC needs to be in the business when the transaction closes. Some buyers may argue that the business needs to have many months of NWC at close. If the seller doesn't have the amount the buyer is demanding, the buyer will try to reduce the deal price to make up for the shortfall. Or, the buyer can use NWC to grab cash in the seller's business that otherwise would be distributed to the seller at close as part of the CF/DF purchase price.

Let's say that the seller has $4 million of cash in the business and no debt. Because the company is being sold on a CF/DF basis, the seller is entitled to take this money at close.

The NWC comes to $1 million a month. The buyer—seeing $4 million of cash in the business—demands that the seller provide enough cash to cover four months of NWC, which just happens to be all the excess cash in the business. If the seller agrees, the buyer has just used NWC to grab a lot of money that would otherwise be kept by the seller.

I've talked to numerous agency owners who've been blindsided by aggressive NWC demands from buyers. Being aware of this negotiating point and understanding how it impacts your deal value will help you prepare in advance to get a good outcome. Most importantly, keep in mind that there's no set definition for the appropriate amount of NWC, as much as the buyer wants you to believe otherwise!

Secured and Unsecured Debt. If the buyer is going to owe you a large amount of money in the future, it's worth understanding whether that payment will be **secured debt** (e.g., the debt is backed by some sort of collateral, such as equipment, real estate, or even the business itself) or unsecured debt (not backed by collateral). Because secured debt is always paid before unsecured debt, in a situation where the buyer doesn't have enough money to pay all of his debts, being a secured debt holder can be the difference between getting paid and getting nothing.

Note: Banks are notorious for insisting that no other creditor be given secured debt as a condition for giving out a business loan. So your acquirer may be contractually prohibited from securing your debt. If your only option is to accept unsecured debt, make sure to research the financial strength of your acquirer carefully. In the event of a bankruptcy, secured debt and employee wages are paid first and unsecured debt is last.

DEAL STRUCTURE

- **Asset or Stock Sale**. An **asset sale** is the purchase of individual assets and liabilities, whereas a **stock sale** is the purchase of the owner's shares of a corporation.

  This distinction largely has tax consequences for both sides. As described by one financial advisor: "Generally, a stock sale is better for the seller, and an asset sale is better for the buyer. In a stock sale, the seller can realize the gain on their business at preferred capital gains tax rates. In an asset sale, any gains are exposed to the seller's ordinary income tax rate on certain assets. If the company is sold as an asset through a C-corp, the proceeds are exposed to double taxation (corporate tax and individual tax rates). The buyer, however, prefers an asset purchase from a tax perspective because they'll have a stepped-up basis which allows for additional depreciation and/or limits the potential gain should the business be sold in the future."[2]

The tax consequences of paying ordinary taxes rather than capital gains can be massive. Currently, the federal capital gains tax rate is 20%, whereas the top ordinary income tax rate is 37%. If you're getting $1 million from a sale, the difference between ordinary income and capital gains is $170,000, and this doesn't include state tax consequences.

Note that it's possible to structure an asset sale in a way that the seller gets capital gains—it just needs to be done properly. So you don't need to outright reject an offer because it's an asset sale, just talk to a competent tax attorney to understand your options.

- **Control and Separation of the Company during Earnout.** If an earnout is part of your deal, there's a good chance that earnout will be contingent on hitting performance milestones. A typical earnout might establish an EBITDA goal over a two- or three-year period. If the seller achieves 100% or more of the goal, the seller gets 100% of the earnout potential. Anything less than that would mean that the seller gets less than 100%.

  From a contract perspective, it's important to clarify how your EBITDA will be measured and kept separate from the acquirer's EBITDA. If your finances are mixed with the buyer's, you run the risk that the buyer gives himself too much credit for revenue and gives you too much credit for costs, which could result in you missing your earnout targets.

---

[2]Marco A. Segrega and Evensky & Katy/Foldes, *Asset Sale vs. Stock Sale: How to Weigh the Options When Selling a Business.* https://evensky.com/news/asset-sale-vs-stock-sale/.

The easiest way to handle this is to keep the two businesses completely separate during the earnout period. This, however, may not be practical for a variety of reasons, so it's crucial to create clear definitions and rules to follow about how financial results are calculated.

Earnout disputes are fairly common when the buyer is a large holding company. The last thing you want is to get to the end of your earnout and be forced to litigate how much you're owed.

INCORPORATION

- **C-corps and Qualified Small Business Stock (QSBS).** Many founders elect to incorporate their agency as an LLC or an S corp. These forms of incorporation are easier to set up and allow for pass-through taxation, meaning that the owners aren't taxed at the corporate level and then again at the personal level when they take dividends. C Corps are harder to set up and manage, and do have double taxation.

  In the event that you did incorporate as a C Corp, there are two important tax consequences you may need to consider upon acquisition. The first is a concept called Qualified Small Business Stock (QSBS). QSBS is a provision of the tax code that may enable you to sell your business and pay no long-term capital gains on the sale. To qualify, your business has to meet several criteria, including being registered as a C Corp for at least five years. The bottom line is to ask your lawyer to investigate whether you might qualify for QSBS and to ensure that the structure of the business post-acquisition doesn't negate your QSBS status.

  The second tax consequence is phantom gain. Phantom gain means that you pay taxes on appreciation of stock from which you've not yet actually received proceeds. This can be triggered when a C Corp is acquired by an LLC.

For example, if a C Corp sells to an LLC for $50 million with a deal structure of $20 million in cash and $30 million in earnouts, the IRS may require the C Corp owners to pay tax on all $50 million of the sales price. If you assume a 20% federal capital gains tax and a 13% state capital gains tax, the founders may be required to pay $16.5 million in taxes upon completion of the sale, leaving them with immediate proceeds of only $3.5 million.

- **State of Incorporation**. Most companies incorporate in the state of Delaware. There are many reasons for this, including tax benefits, a corporation court system to handle disputes, fast filing processes, and the simple fact that most lawyers are very familiar with the system. Don't be surprised or alarmed if the company buying you is or wants to be incorporated in Delaware.

  On the other hand, if the buyer wants to incorporate outside of Delaware, you may want to dig deeper. Sometimes there's a perfectly good reason for selecting another state in which to incorporate (for example, this may be where the buyer is headquartered and is already incorporated there). In other cases, the decision to incorporate in another state is driven by favorable laws that might benefit the acquirer and hurt your business. For example, in Delaware, it's presumed that a board member has a **fiduciary duty** to protect the interests of shareholders (meaning they must act as if they're in the shoes of the shareholder). In Nevada, by contrast, it's presumed that there's *no* fiduciary duty unless explicitly included in the language of the contract. As we'll discuss later, fiduciary duty is an important concept that protects the rights of minority shareholders (like you!).

EMPLOYMENT CONTRACTS

Buyers normally require key employees (especially executives!) to sign employment contracts as part of the acquisition process. On the surface, this is not a reason to become alarmed. That said, an overly restrictive or punitive employment contract can create liabilities and risks in the future. Here are some of the key points to negotiate in an employment contract:

- **Non-Competes and Non-Solicitations**. It's common for an acquirer to demand that the key employees of the seller agency refrain from working at a competitor (through a **non-compete agreement**) or trying to recruit clients or employees to work with another company, regardless of whether this is or is not a competitor of the acquirer (through a **non-solicitation agreement**). If an employee violates one of these clauses, the acquirer may sue for damages, and the employee could be personally liable to pay the acquirer for such damages.

  As a starting point to negotiating these clauses, it's in the best interest of the seller to define a "competitor" and a "solicitation" as narrowly as possible. So, for example, instead of a clause that says a competitor is "any company that offers agency services," a better clause for the seller might read "any company that offers search engine optimization services to financial services companies located in the United States."

  Secondly, non-competes and non-solicits should have the shortest time period possible. The length of these clauses is usually either defined from the date of the acquisition or from the date that the employee leaves the company. Generally, I would say that a non-compete/non-solicit of two years is a reasonable request.

  That said, how much compensation each employee is getting from the deal will have an impact. For example, assume a buyer wants the CEO, head of sales, and head of client services to each sign a two-year non-compete. The CEO gets paid $500,000 a year and will make $10 million on the transaction, while the two other leaders each make $250,000 a year and will make $300,000 on the transaction. For the CEO, a two-year non-compete isn't a big deal. He would have to give up $1 million of salary, but he has made $10 million on the deal. The other two leaders, however, are being asked to give up $500,000 of compensation while only making $300,000 on the deal. In other words, they're losing money. This would be unfair and worth trying to negotiate. One solution may be to require the CEO to sign up for a much longer non-compete and have the other executives take a much shorter one.

Another important point about non-competes: In many states (like California), non-competes are "on their face" invalid, meaning that even if an employee signs one, it's still unenforceable. The caveat to these laws is that they generally don't apply to employees who are selling equity in a transaction (i.e., they become enforceable upon these employees).

- **Termination**. What happens if you resign or get fired from the company? In some cases, the proposed language of the contract may state that you lose the entire value of your remaining equity.

Generally, there are three ways an employee leaves a company: they resign, they're fired *without cause*, or they're fired *with cause*. Being fired without cause means leaving on good terms with the company. In most cases, this is the result of a layoff or unsatisfactory job performance. Being fired for cause, however, means that you violated your employment contract, broke a law, or otherwise did something that harmed the company. In this instance, the seller may put language in your employment contract that forces you to sell back your stock to the company at cost, which may mean that you lose the entire value of your equity!

The other major factor in a termination clause is the amount of severance to which you're entitled. It's not uncommon for a founder to get six months to one year of severance, but this is always negotiable.

In general, your goal is to preserve as many rights as possible if you leave the company—in particular, your board seats, your rights around stock repurchase, your stock class, and amount of equity.

MINORITY RIGHTS

As the owner of your business, you're used to having the final say in most decisions. Once you sell, you lose this right and instead must defer to the majority owner on most decisions. This can feel scary, especially if the decisions could have a negative impact on the value of your stock or earnout. For this reason, it's important to add "minority rights" to the contract—terms that limit the majority from making important decisions without your input or approval.

- **Fiduciary Duty.** A fiduciary duty requires that an investor treat someone else's stock in the same way as they would treat their own. In Delaware, there's a presumption of a fiduciary duty. It doesn't need to be explicitly mentioned in a contract (but that shouldn't prevent you from demanding that it is included). It's also possible for a contract to include a clause that explicitly waives that fiduciary duty.

  Here's why it's important to have this clause in your contract. Let's say that after you sell the company, the buyer gets an offer from a new buyer to acquire the business. The deal is worth $537.5 million and pays Class A shareholders (the buyers) $20 a share, and pays Class B shareholders (you) $1.50 a share. Prior to the deal, you held 25 million shares of Class B stock at a value of $1 per share, representing 50% of the company value, and the buyers held 25 million shares of Class A at a value of $1 per share, also representing 50% of the company value. In this deal, however, the buyers get $500 million of the proceeds and you get $37.5 million.

TABLE 8-I: Stock Class Valuations			
COMPANY FORMATION STOCK VALUES			
	UNITS	PRICE PER UNIT	VALUE
Class A	25000000	$ 1.0	$ 25,000,000
Class B	25000000	$ 1.0	$ 25,000,000
TOTAL	50000000	$	$ 50,000,000

PURCHASE TERMS OFFERED BY ACQUIRER			
	UNITS	PRICE PER UNIT	VALUE
Class A	25000000	$ 20.0	$ 500,000,000
Class B	25000000	$ 1.5	$ 37,500,000
TOTAL	50000000	$	$ 537,500,000

This is a great deal for your buyers, but if they put themselves in your shoes, there's no way they would ever sign this deal. If they have a fiduciary duty to look out for your interests, they would almost certainly be prohibited from agreeing to such an offer. In fact, the above example is so extreme that even without a fiduciary duty, a court would likely invalidate it. The point, however, remains: Get the buyer to agree to a fiduciary duty if possible.

- **Pari-Passu. Pari-passu** means "on the same footing." If you're pari-passu with your buyer, it means that you have the same rights as the buyer. This is a good thing to request!

- **Right to Repurchase.** In any contract that involves an equity rollover or stock option plan, the **right to repurchase** stock is one of the most important clauses in the contract. Imagine, for example, a company that sells for $50 million, with $25 million in cash up front and $25 million in rollover stock. The contract states that the buyer can elect to repurchase the founders' stock for **fair market value (FMV)** and that the buyer can determine the FMV based on "reasonable market comparables." The business does really well after the acquisition, so much so that the sellers believe that the company is now worth $200 million. Yet one day, they get a letter from the buyer notifying them that all of the seller's stock is being repurchased by the buyer with a valuation of just $75 million. They support this valuation by sharing an analysis performed by an accounting firm the buyer hired. The sellers have no choice but to accept the offer. One year later, the company is sold for $300 million.

  When thinking about a right to repurchase clause, here are the primary points on which to focus:

  - **What Can Trigger a Repurchase?** In most cases, a founder must voluntarily leave or be fired for the company to repurchase his shares. The best case for the founder is that there's no trigger, e.g., the company doesn't have a right to compel the founder to sell shares back. They can make an offer, but the founder can reject it for any reason. Often, a compromise is made where the company can repurchase stock only if the founder is fired for cause (the definition of "fired for cause" should be made clear in your employment agreement).

– **When is the Founder Paid?** Some contracts give the company the right to pay for a stock repurchase over a long period of time. There might be a clause in the contract that allows for the company to pay the founder with a note due in the distant future. In this scenario, the company locks in a repurchase right at the value today, but then pays the founder in the future when the company is worth much more (and the time-value of money has reduced the payment value).

– **How is the Fair Market Value (FMV) Determined?** It's difficult and subjective to determine the value of a privately held company. As such, if you sign a contract that allows the company to unilaterally determine the value of your stock, you will inevitably get less than you think the company is worth (even if the company is acting in good faith).

The fairest way to determine FMV that I've discovered is called **baseball arbitration**. It works like this: An arbitrator is hired by both parties to determine the FMV of the stock being repurchased. Each side can present their estimation of FMV to the arbitrator. Here's the catch: The arbitrator cannot split the difference down the middle. He must choose one of the proposals.

The result of baseball arbitration is that both parties are incentivized to be reasonable. Imagine that your company is worth somewhere between $75 million and $100 million. You present a valuation estimate to the arbitrator of $92 million—toward the high end of the range. The company, by contrast, makes an offer of $35 million—way below the likely range. The arbitrator must choose one of the offers and decides to pick your number, because you were the most reasonable.

- **Can the Founder Receive Less than FMV?** There are instances where a contract will give the company the right to buy back shares for less than the current FMV. If the founder is fired for cause (i.e., he did something egregiously bad like commit fraud), the company may put in a clause that gives the company the right to buy back the founder's stock at cost. "At cost" can mean the value of the stock when the agency was acquired, or it can mean the par value of the stock when it was issued (which may be a nominal amount, like $.01 a share). In either case, not getting FMV can result in millions of lost value for a founder.

- **Tag-Along Rights**. A minority shareholder with **tag-along rights** has the right to sell his shares for the same price and terms as the majority investor. In other words, the majority investor can't sign a deal to sell just his shares (perhaps at a fat profit) and refuse to let the minority shareholder also benefit from that sale.

LIABILITY

- **Indemnification**. When you indemnify someone, you agree to compensate someone else for losses that they have incurred or will incur as related to a specified incident. A common indemnification is tax indemnification—if a buyer purchases your agency and then is subject to an IRS audit of the pre-acquisition date range, if the buyer has tax indemnification, you must cover the costs and fines associated with this audit.

  There are a couple of big "gotchas" to be aware of with respect to indemnification clauses. First, it's important to note that some indemnification clauses ask for personal indemnification, meaning that you and your fellow founders are financially on the hook for these indemnification claims. This is a clause that you should strongly resist. You incorporated in the first place in part to shield yourself from personal liability, so why would you open yourself up to exposure now?

Second, beware of overly broad indemnification clauses. For example, an indemnification clause that holds you liable for "all lawsuits or claims brought against the company that transpired prior to the acquisition" holds you responsible for everything that happened in the past, even though you were not aware of it and couldn't have prevented it. A more reasonable clause would only hold the seller liable in cases where the seller knew or should have known of a claim.

- **Representations (Reps) and Warranties**. Representations and warranties are statements made by one party to another in a contract, typically as part of a sales or acquisition agreement. Representations are factual statements about a party's current condition, knowledge, or intentions, while warranties are promises that certain conditions will be met or maintained. Representations and warranties serve as a basis for the parties to rely upon in their agreement, and they help to ensure that the transaction is completed as expected. If a representation or warranty is later found to be false, the other party may have the right to terminate the contract or seek compensation.

  Common reps and warranties you may be asked to agree include:

  - **Employee Matters**. You represent that you have properly dealt with all employee-related matters, including the payment of all compensation and benefits, and that there are no pending or threatened claims related to employees.

- **Financial Statements**. You represent that your financial statements accurately reflect its financial condition and that you have not omitted any material information.

- **Intellectual Property**. You represent that you own or have the right to use all of the intellectual property being sold, and that there are no pending or threatened claims related to intellectual property

- **Litigation**. You represent that there are no pending or threatened lawsuits or claims that would have a material impact on the assets or shares being sold.

- **Material Contracts**. You represent that you're not a party to any material contracts that would be affected by the sale, and that you have not received any notice of default under any material contract.

- **Organizational Status and Authority**. You have the legal authority to enter into the contract and complete the sale.

- **Ownership and Title**. You own the assets or shares being sold, and that they're free and clear of any liens or encumbrances.

- **Taxes**. You represent that you have satisfied all of your tax obligations and that there are no tax liabilities that would be assumed by the buyer as a result of the sale.

If you're an honest broker and have disclosed all potential problems to the buyer during due diligence, none of these should be too worrisome to approve. That said, an aggressive buyer may attempt to use reps and warranties to hold you responsible for problems that you didn't even know existed at the time of signature.

For example, let's say that the buyer includes a rep that says that you're responsible for paying for any future litigation caused by actions taken by your company prior to selling the business. Two years after your deal closes, a disgruntled ex-employee sues the company, claiming he was wrongfully terminated six months before you signed the deal. The employee did not make this claim when he was terminated, so there's no way you could have disclosed this to the seller. The seller now wants you to pay for the claim out of your pocket!

There are two things you can do to prevent this sort of surprise liability from occurring. First, limit reps and warranties to existing, known liabilities. Second, set a time limit on how long the buyer has to make a claim against you for a breach.

AFTER THE DEAL IS COMPLETE, SELLING THE BUSINESS AGAIN, OR RAISING MONEY

In the movie *The Social Network*—about the founding of Facebook— there's a key scene where Mark Zuckerberg informs his co-founder Eduardo Saverin that his stock is being reduced in value by about one hundred times (making his $3 billion of stock worth about $30 million!). Unfortunately, this sort of "reverse split" or stock devaluation can happen if the right terms aren't inserted into the contract.

- **Additional Funding Rounds**. Under what circumstances can the buyers of your agency raise new funds? Can they **"cram down"** previous rounds of investors? A cram down is when a new round gets favorable terms that reduce the value of the past round. This normally happens when the business has declined in value and the new investors demand a lower valuation or additional preferences? Do you have the right to maintain your **pro rata** (percentage ownership) of the company if you choose to invest in the new round?

- **Change of Control**. If the buyers want to sell the company or merge with another company, what rights do you have to object to this sale? Will you be treated pari-passu (the same) with your investors when the deal closes?

- **Drag-Along Rights**. A **drag-along** right gives the majority owner the right to force the minority to join in the sale of the company. In other words, it forces the minority to vote for the sale of the company, even though they might have preferred to not sell the company. As a general rule, investors want the board to vote unanimously for a sale—anything less can make an acquirer nervous about future lawsuits. So the drag-along forces the minority to join the majority in a unanimous vote.

  Under Delaware **common law** (common law means established general principles that do not need to be in the contract to be enforced), drag-alongs cannot specifically and adversely treat minority shareholders differently than the majority. That said, remember the best practice—get it in writing! If you see a drag-along right, add a clause that reinforces your common law right, like: "No amendment to this Agreement that would disproportionately, materially and adversely affect the minority shareholders shall be effective against the minority shareholders without the written consent of the minority shareholders."

STOCK

Unless you're receiving an all cash offer (which is rare), or cash plus an earnout (which is common with Hold Cos, but less so with other buyers), part of the consideration you will get for selling your agency will be stock in the acquirer or a newly formed entity.

- **Stock Classes**. There are generally up to two types of stock: preferred and common. Preferred stock has two advantages over common stock. First, the preferred stock gets paid first before the common. Second, the preferred usually gets a PIK. Preferred stock may also have additional rights (like information rights and tag-along rights). Needless to say, if your buyer is creating a structure with preferred shares, you want your shares to be preferred.

- **Preferred Return (PIK)**. In private equity deals (which includes being bought by a private equity company and being bought by an agency owned by a private equity company), it's common for the investors to receive a preferred return (known as a PIK) on their investment.

  Here is how this works. Assume that a company is bought for $100 million and that the investors own $80 million of the company after acquisition, and the founders own $20 million. The investors write a payment in kind (PIK) into the contract that pays them an annual 10% interest payment (compounding) until the company is sold.

  It takes five years to sell the company, and the sales price is $150 million. The investors get $62 million in **preferred return**, leaving $88 million to be split up. They then get 80% of the remainder ($70.6 million), leaving $17.7 million for the founders. In other words, because of the interest from the PIK, the investors $80 million initial investment ballooned to $132.4 million but the founders $20 million actually declined to $17.7 million!

TABLE 8-2: Without Preferred Return

WITHOUT PREFERRED RETURN

	At Close	Year 1	Year 2	Year 3	Year 4	Year 5	TOTAL
Investor Equity Percentage	80%	80%	80%	80%	80%	80%	
Founder Equity Percentage	20%	20%	20%	20%	20%	20%	
Sale of Business						$ 150,000,000	
Investor 80% Equity Payout						$ 120,000,000	
Founder 20% Equity Payout						$ 30,000,000	
TOTAL to Investors						$ 120,000,000	
TOTAL to Founders						$ 30,000,000	

TABLE 8-3: With Preferred Return

	At Close	Year 1	Year 2	Year 3	Year 4	Year 5	TOTAL
Investor Equity Percentage	80%	80%	80%	80%	80%	80%	
Annual Compounding Preferred Return of 10%	$ 8,000,000	$ 8,800,000	$ 9,680,000	$ 10,648,000	$ 11,712,800	$ 12,884,080	$ 61,724,880
Founder Equity Percentage	20%	20%	20%	20%		20%	
Sale of Business						$ 150,000,000	
Investor Preferred Return						$ 61,724,880	
Remaining Payout						$ 88,275,120	
Investor 80% Equity Payout						$ 70,620,096	
Founder 20% Equity Payout						$ 17,655,024	
TOTAL to Investors						$ 132,344,976	
TOTAL to Founders						$ 17,655,024	

There are two ways of dealing with preferred returns. First, you can argue that no one—investors, founders, or employees—should get preferred returns. And second, you can argue that founders should join investors in getting preferred returns. Obviously, the second solution can feel a little like you're abandoning your employees. One argument in favor of founders getting preferred stock and not giving this right to employees is that founders took a risk in founding the business and employees took much less risk—the more risk, the more return. Ultimately, this is a decision that every founding team has to make for themselves.

One other note: I've seen contracts that attempt to create a "heads I win, tails you lose" situation for founders when it comes to preferred stock. The argument the buyer makes against giving the founders preferred stock is that the founder is getting a lot of cash compensation in the sale, so she is really more like an employee than an investor. When, however, it comes time to issue stock options to the team, the investors argue that the founders already have a lot of equity in the company and thus shouldn't participate in the stock option program. In other words, the buyer treats the founder like an employee when convenient and like an investor when convenient, resulting in both less valuable stock and less overall stock for the founder.

• **Stock Option Plans**. In many deals, it's common to carve out some of the company equity as a stock option plan for employees. Typically, this amounts to somewhere between five and ten percent of the common stock. As a founder, you can often insert yourself into the stock option plan. As CEO, you may be able to get between one and three percent of the company in stock options. To be clear, this is above and beyond the rollover stock you already have. This is a great thing to negotiate after you have agreed on valuation and the rollover.

- **Stock Ownership**. When you sell your agency, you will often get stock in either the buyer's company or the newly formed corporation created as a result of the agency sale. This stock does not need to vest—you get it immediately after the deal closes. You also don't have to buy it—you paid for it when you sold your agency—and the stock is typically the same class of stock as the acquirer.

  Contrast this to a stock option plan—which requires vesting and stock purchase and is often a class of stock that's inferior to that of the acquirers.

- **Stock Vesting and Acceleration**. Common stock option plans will always include a vesting schedule, such that every quarter or year that you're at the company, you get more and more of your stock. A typical plan might include a four-year vesting period with monthly vesting after the first year of employment. Obviously, if you can negotiate a shorter vesting period, you'll get your stock more quickly.

  The other factor to negotiate is **stock vesting acceleration**. In a change of control (usually a sale), most stock plans call for some or all of the stock to accelerate from unvested to vested. In a perfect world, you should demand that 100% of your stock is accelerated upon a change of control.

OTHER

- **Check the Math**. In one of the sales of 3Q, our earnout was contingent on the CAGR of the business. Recall that CAGR is a measure of the average annual growth rate of the business.

In the contract, the buyer's attorneys added an equation to calculate CAGR and then spelled out the equation in words.

A few months after we closed the deal, we took a closer look at the contract and realized that the definition of CAGR in the document was not the *average* annual growth rate, but the *aggregate* annual growth rate. This meant that—even if we barely grew the business—we were virtually guaranteed to achieve the full earnout.

One thing that courts look at in deciding a lawsuit is whether both sides were represented by competent legal counsel. When the court concludes this is the case, the court presumes that whatever was written in the document must have been the intent of the parties. In our case, because the buyer had expert attorneys from a very large firm (in fact, while they were working on our deal, other parts of the firm were representing the President!), the argument that they had added the wrong equation would hold no merit. As it turns out, we hit the target for the standard definition of CAGR, too, so the point was moot.

The moral of this story is to check the contract—and especially financial figures and equations—multiple times. Don't assume that your $1000 an hour lawyers are good at inserting numbers correctly into the contract!

- You might sign your car rental agreement without reading the small print, but you absolutely should *not* take that approach to M&A contracts. Years from now—perhaps when your buyer is considering selling the business again or your earnout is due—there's a good chance that the people you signed your deal with will have moved on to other companies. The people who've taken their place may not have been with the company when your deal was signed. They may or may not be good, ethical people either.

- Inevitably disputes arise—even in the most perfect deals—and the first thing lawyers, executives, and courts will look to in determining the rights of the parties are the contractual documents (the four corners of the document). Spending a few extra weeks or even months on high-priced lawyers and creating documents that protect your minority interests, create a fair board, put you pari-passu with your investors, define financial outcomes, and clarify your rights and responsibilities is crucial.

RECOMMENDED READING

- *Never Split the Difference: Negotiating As If Your Life Depended On It*, by Chris Voss and Tahl Raz

- *Thinking in Bets: Making Smart Decisions When You Don't Have All the Facts*, by Annie Duke

CHAPTER NINE

THE DEAL IS SIGNED, NOW WHAT?

It's a strange feeling to login to your bank account and suddenly see a bunch of zeros behind the "Account Balance" dollar amount for the first time. I'm not going to lie. I took a screenshot and showed it to my brother (Note: I live in California, so the number was a lot bigger than the final amount, after California and federal taxes!).

You can and should celebrate this momentous event. Take a day or two off to recuperate. Selling an agency is an exhausting experience and sharing a bottle of wine with the executive team or taking your spouse to a nice restaurant should be part of the post-deal process.

But . . . once you've let off some steam, there's still a lot of work left to be done. The sad truth is that a lot of M&A deals actually fail to meet the expectations of both the buyer and seller. So creating a post-purchase plan to announce the deal and integrate the company into the buyer's organization is crucial.

CREATING A COMMUNICATION STRATEGY

Ultimately, there are three key stakeholders who you will need to "sell" on the deal: staff, clients, and everyone else (general PR). In a perfect world, you want to control the message in terms of who hears the news when, and you want everyone who learns about the deal to view it in a positive light.

Once you have a high degree of confidence that your deal is a few weeks from closing, you should start creating the communications strategy. You don't necessarily have to announce the deal at the exact moment the legal contracts are signed, but it's a good idea to make the announcement as soon as you can, so giving yourself a couple of weeks of lead time is important.

The key members of the deal communication team are the CEO, head of marketing, PR team or agency (if these exist), head of client services, and the same set of people and teams at the buyer's firm or agency. In most deals, all of these parties have been aware of the deal for many months, so there's no need to tell more people about the transaction.

The communications plan should include the following elements:

- Lists of groups of people you need to tell about the deal, when you plan to tell them, what you will tell them, and who will tell them.

- Updates to your website and marketing collateral with the announcement, email footer, business cards, and any changes to branding or naming.

- A PR strategy to get positive media coverage from trade media and national media.

- FAQs and talking points for all employees.

- A schedule of when different parts of the plan will be delivered.

TELLING YOUR TEAM ABOUT THE SALE

As a general point, you want all parties to be notified at around the same time, simply because secrets are hard to keep. The more people who know about the deal, the more likely it is that an important person or partner will find out about the deal before you formally tell them (which could mean that the message is not fully communicated, or the partner becomes angry that they were not among the first to know).

Change is difficult for most people.
You can spin the most rosy tale of how the
sale of the agency is going to be a huge win
for everyone at the company, but inevitably
there will be some team members who are
scared, angry, or confused.

That being said, the first group to notify is usually your team. This is mainly because your team will be the ones notifying most of your clients, so they need to have the right talking points. After the team is informed, clients are next, followed by the general public last. In most cases, this is done over a 12- to 24-hour period.

Change is difficult for most people. You can spin the most rosy tale of how the sale of the agency is going to be a huge win for everyone at the company, but inevitably there will be some team members who are scared, angry, or confused. Do your best, but don't expect the entire team to respond positively to the news.

My approach to telling team members is to do a "cascading communication." Start with any executives who have yet to be informed (at this point, there shouldn't be many), then inform managers, and then inform the team. Generally, executives and managers are told the night before the acquisition announcement, and team members are told concurrently with the press release announcing the deal. Note that by "manager" I don't mean anyone who has "manager" in their title, but rather senior leaders in the organization who manage many people. In a 100-person client services team, this might mean between 10 and 15 people.

Your first meeting with executives and managers is an opportunity to refine the messaging you will tell to the rest of the staff—so listen closely for any confusion or concerns and adjust your presentation accordingly for the next series of meetings!

For your two meetings with execs and with managers, start by sending a meeting invite to each group to whom you're going to talk. The meeting title should say something like "Mandatory and Confidential Meeting." In the meeting description, add something like this: "Please join us this evening for an important meeting. This is a mandatory meeting. Cancel all other meetings other than absolutely critical client meetings (email me if this is the case). Please do not tell anyone (employees, family, or your personal trainer) about this meeting."

At the meeting, start by announcing the deal in an honest and positive way. For example, you might say:

> As you know, we've had a phenomenal year. We've won some amazing clients. We've been able to double the size of the business, enter into new service areas, and win several important industry awards. Suffice to say, all of this success has been noticed by partners and competitors. Earlier this year, we were getting calls almost weekly from companies that wanted to either merge with us, invest in us, or outright buy us. We listened to all

of these companies, but we rejected almost all of them, simply because the deals they were proposing didn't meet our three core principles: good for our team, good for our clients, good for our shareholders.

Then, in May, we met XYZ Corp. We were immediately struck by how their culture was similar to ours. And we loved the fact that they offered A, B, and C services to their clients (which we don't), and we offered D, E, and F services to our clients (which they don't). It just felt like putting our two companies together was a "two plus two equals five" opportunity.

And that's why I'm excited to tell you that we're merging with XYZ. The deal will be announced tomorrow.

Next, transition to why the deal is positive for the team. This could be anything from the potential for better client results, opportunities to learn new skills, relocation possibilities to cool cities, or better benefits and compensation. In one of 3Q's deals, the company with whom we were merging hosted an annual three-day party in Europe for all employees—that was very well received by the team!

An important note: If some of your team has equity and others don't, it's best not to discuss the value of the equity (or even the value of the deal) at this juncture. These discussions should be done one-on-one with equity holders.

Lastly, provide the team with a script and frequently asked questions (FAQ) for talking to their staff and to clients. Ideally, the executive or manager should not read the script verbatim, but should discuss it in their own personal style.

The FAQ should answer questions that you anticipate staff or clients will ask. A best practice is to create separate FAQs for staff and clients.

Common staff questions include:

- Why did we do this now? Aren't we growing?
- Will anyone be laid off?
- Will any benefits be taken away?
- Are any execs leaving?
- Will I be reporting to someone new?
- Does the new company offer stock options?
- What are the terms of the deal? (As a general rule, contract details should *not* be discussed.)
- Is this an acquisition?
- Are we still independent?
- What does this mean for my job?
- What does this mean for my clients?
- What does this mean for my budget?
- Are we keeping our offices?
- Do our business goals change?

At this point, open the floor to questions. Hopefully, most questions asked will have already been addressed in the FAQs. If not, consider adding relevant questions to the FAQ as they arise.

After all questions are answered, reiterate to the team they need to keep this confidential.

If your executive/senior leadership team is small enough and located in the same city, this may also be a good time to have a celebratory dinner!

Next, schedule your all-hands meeting to tell the entire company. Ideally, your executive/manager meeting should be held the night before the public announcement of the acquisition. Your all-hands meeting should be scheduled immediately before or concurrently with the public announcement. Thus, if you're making a 9 a.m. EST announcement, your all-hands meeting should be at either 8 a.m. or 9 a.m. EST.

The content of the presentation to the staff should basically be the same as for your executive and manager meetings. You may also want to offer a series of open office hours meetings with the leadership staff in the days after the initial announcement. This allows team members time to process the news and ask more questions.

3Q had numerous offices across the country. We felt it was important to have an executive at each office on the announcement day, and thus we flew executives to offices that didn't have a local executive so we had someone in person to respond to any concerns from the staff in that office. We also flew a representative of the acquirer (either the CEO or a partner with the PE firm) to our largest office to jointly announce the news and then host a happy hour to have a chance for staff members to meet the acquirer in an informal setting.

TELLING CLIENTS ABOUT THE SALE

The majority of your clients should be contacted by their account manager soon after the announcement of the sale. The account manager should rely on the script/FAQ to share the news with the client. If there are questions or concerns that the client has that she cannot address, these should be immediately sent up the chain of command so someone higher in the organization can follow up with the client.

To paraphrase *Animal Farm*, all clients are equal, but some clients are more equal than others. For your most important clients, the news of the acquisition should be communicated on multiple levels. For example, an executive at your company who already works with the client should reach out to the most senior person they know at the client to let them know the news (usually the CMO for a large client or the CEO for a smaller client). The account team should concurrently follow up with the day-to-day client contacts.

In some cases, you may even want to let your most important clients know about the deal the day before the announcement. This makes them feel special and strengthens your relationship during what would otherwise be a time of some uncertainty.

It may feel scary telling clients about such a big change. In my experience, 95% of clients have a positive reaction to acquisition news. As long as their day-to-day experience with your agency doesn't change (e.g., same team, same service, same contract), clients don't dwell much on these sorts of announcements.

Common client questions include:

- Will my team change?
- How does this affect my contract? (in some cases, a "change of control" clause in the contract allows the client to cancel immediately if they so desire.)
- Does the new company work with any of my competitors?
- Will there be any changes to pricing or fee structure?
- Will the agency be merging with the acquirer or operating independently?
- Are any execs leaving?

DEVELOPING A PR STRATEGY

The last prong of your communications strategy is to get positive news coverage from the press. For most agency M&A, PR is not that important, simply because your deal may be a big deal to you, but it really isn't that newsworthy to the rest of the world. A 100-person agency acquiring a 20-person agency isn't going to attract the attention of the *Wall Street Journal*. Moreover, few potential prospects are going to suddenly decide to reach out to you as a result of learning that you just sold your business. For the most part, PR is really about assuring your existing clients and staff that the deal is legitimate.

With that in mind, here are some tips to get good coverage for your announcement. First, write a blog post. Press releases are predictable and dry (and thus don't get shared or picked up by news outlets). A great blog post—one that's personal, detailed, and thoughtful—can get you a lot of free coverage.

Ideally, you're already a great writer and can write this in your voice. If writing isn't your thing, consider hiring an executive blogger who has experience ghost-writing posts for company leaders.

When we sold 3Q to Harte Hanks in 2015, I wrote an extensive blog post[1] announcing the decision to sell and explaining the rationale behind it. Here's the outline of that post:

- A brief history of 3Q.

- The three requirements that had to be met before we decided to sell.

  – Is this good for clients?

  – Is this good for team members?

  – Is this a smart financial decision?

---

[1] https://www.3qdept.com/blog/harte-hanks-acquires-3q-digital-read-the-inside-story-here/.

- Why merging with Harte Hanks is a win for all constituents.

  – Customers wanted integrated marketing.

  – Agencies need to be technology intermediaries.

  – We need to offer both services and tech.

- What's next and thank you!

The second PR idea is to offer a major news outlet an exclusive on the announcement. This means pitching the story to a few news sources that normally wouldn't cover your deal but might be tempted if you gave them an exclusive. This usually happens about a week before the announcement and requires the news outlet to agree to a **media embargo** (they won't publish the story until the press release goes live).

The key here is to aim high but not too high. Again, the *Wall Street Journal* is unlikely to cover any agency sales under about $1 billion of value, so even an exclusive isn't going to get you coverage. That said, a trade publication like *AdAge* or *Adweek* might devote more space to your deal if they get an exclusive.

Third, encourage your team to spread the news on social media, in particular business-focused sites like LinkedIn and Twitter.

Next, designate an official spokesperson. In the event that any press reach out, make sure everyone knows to connect the media to this person.

Lastly, send out a press release. This is a necessary but generally pointless endeavor—few people read press releases other than your PR agency and your parents!

CREATING AN INTEGRATION PLAN

A few days after our first sale closed, the Chief HR Officer of our acquirer appeared in our offices and summarily announced to me and my executive team that he was in charge of all operations at 3Q effective immediately. This was a shock for three reasons: First, because the CEO had assured us that he wanted us to continue operating as an independent executive team. Second, because we had already developed a comprehensive integration plan—approved by our acquirer—that clearly delineated roles and responsibilities. Third, because the acquisition contract clearly stated that we would continue to run operations (and finance, marketing, sales, HR, client services, and IT) until after our earnout was completed.

Put another way, prior to the deal closing, we had established a meeting of the minds, a plan, and a clear contract that resolved any misunderstandings. You can see how an integration would fail if just one of these factors was missing. Imagine, for example, that we had a clear integration plan, but we didn't have legal documents to back us up. In that case, the CEO would be forced to decide between honoring his verbal contract to us and angering one of his executives.

As I noted earlier, many acquisitions fail and a lack of planning and alignment on integration is one of the primary fault points (failing to plan is planning to fail!).

There are really two types of integration: operational (using the same payroll systems, setting up email addresses, aligning benefits, creating a new org chart, choosing a common banking partner, etc.) and cultural (building teams across the two organizations, fusing cultures, defining the vision, etc.).

Here are some strategies to make your integration as smooth as possible.

SET UP AN INTEGRATION TEAM

Pre-closing, set up a team of leaders on both sides of the deal to work on integration. This will likely be your entire executive team and the functional equivalents on the acquirer side. This likely means the CEO, CFO, COO, CMO, CHRO, Chief Client Services Officer, and CTO/CPO for your agency. If the company to which you're selling is much larger than you, you may be dealing with Vice Presidents on the other side of the project. Remember that as few people as possible should know about the deal before it's announced, so it's best to limit the integration team at this point to your executives who are already aware of the transaction.

This team should have a regular cadence (at least weekly) that starts before the deal closes and continues for months afterwards. The team should create a laundry list of all the integration tasks that need to be done and assign deliverables and due dates to the appropriate team members.

Note that if you're being acquired by a private equity firm, much less integration is needed. The main integration that needs to take place would be financial—changing your bank to the bank that the PE firm uses.

IT DOESN'T ALL NEED TO GET DONE ON DAY ONE

In every deal I've done, the last month of negotiations has been exhausting. There's always something that doesn't go as planned—the sides get into a prolonged dispute on a contractual term, an approval from a lender takes longer than expected, or a minority shareholder refuses to sign a document.

Whatever the distraction, the result is that the two management teams have to devote their attention to putting out fires to get the deal done, rather than planning for life post-deal. As such, despite your best intentions, it's unlikely that you will have a fully baked integration plan on the day you close and announce the deal.

As long as you accept this—and message it to the team accordingly—this is normal and OK. Will the company implode if the buyer and seller use different payroll systems for the first six months of the deal? Of course not, though the Accounts Payable teams may have to work extra hours!

Of course, you should get as much done as you can before the deal closes, but don't expect an immediate and perfect union of the two companies instantly. Indeed, an argument could be made that keeping the two companies separate for a few months is not a bad strategy. This separation allows the two teams to slowly and smartly integrate and reduces the trepidation that some team members will have about change by gradually integrating.

FIND EARLY SHARED WINS

Many people are afraid of change and will assume the worst whenever change happens. A merger or an acquisition is a major change, and some of your staff will instinctively look at the deal from a glass half-empty perspective.

Come up with reasons for the two teams to work together in a low-stress, positive way that breaks down walls and creates good energy about the transaction.

A good way to build positive energy around the deal is to create projects that create early wins for both teams. For example, if the two teams are going to be working out of the same office, create a committee that's composed of people from both companies to determine the seating chart (and make sure that part of their directive is that they must mix the teams rather than keep them separated!). Once the new seating chart is live, have an office-wide party to celebrate.

In a perfect world, you would also find clients that need services from both teams and immediately combine employees from each company on an actual client project.

The bottom line: Come up with reasons for the two teams to work together in a low-stress, positive way that breaks down walls and creates good energy about the transaction.

MIX THE TEAMS

When we acquired iSearchMedia in 2014, I initially decided to keep iSearch and 3Q teams separate. I reasoned that it would be more productive to have team members continue to work with other people with whom they already had a high level of comfort and good workflows.

This was a mistake. A month after the deal closed, I started to hear a lot of "us versus them" comments. Things like, "The iSearch team isn't as advanced at Google advertising as we are," or "3Q's hiring processes aren't as good as ours at iSearch." This was not constructive criticism—it was tribalism. I realized that the benefits of keeping teams together were offset by the potential of disunity and in-fighting.

Part of the integration strategy should be to create bonds between the two teams and break up any tribal loyalty. This can include:

- A new org chart (with leaders from both teams getting prominent roles, as opposed to only giving major roles to the acquiring company).
- A new seating chart with the teams mixed.
- Team building exercises.
- After-work mixers.

EXPECT SOME BUMPS

No merger or acquisition ever works out exactly as the leaders intended. It's often the case that there's too much over-emphasis on the potential synergies of a deal and too little focus on the potential problems.

Mistakes happen, some strategies don't pan out, and unexpected (and bad) surprises will materialize.

If you expect perfection in M&A, you'll be disappointed. It's important to differentiate between small setbacks and major problems. Conflict between team members, losing some clients that you thought were secure, integration of finances and HR taking longer than expected, not being able to upsell new services as much as expected—these are all disappointing but also within the range of expected outcomes in any deal.

In most deals, these bad results are counterbalanced by above-average outcomes in other areas of the integration. If you're looking for problems and fail to also recognize unexpected wins, you will be perpetually unhappy.

In rare instances, there may be a major problem that's discovered after the deal closes. Perhaps, prior to the deal closing, the acquiring agency had been notified by a major client that they were losing the business, thus substantially reducing the value of the equity they were offering to the acquired agency. Or the financial reports provided during due diligence were fraudulent.

In these situations, go back to the contract you signed, in particular the sections on "representations and warranties." In most cases, both parties want to find a way to keep the deal alive, if possible. The aggrieved party may ask for damages, demand that a key executive be fired for cause, or redistribute equity as a way to cure the problem.

All of these solutions are painful, but they enable the two companies to move forward without completely jettisoning the deal.

KEY TAKEAWAYS FROM THIS CHAPTER

- Creating a communications plan and an integration plan are foundational requirements for a successful merger or acquisition. The communication plan has three stakeholders: employees, clients, and everyone else. Create a cascading communication plan, starting with executives, then senior management, then all other employees. Most employees should be notified the night before the deal is announced or concurrently with the public announcement.

- Create FAQs and scripts for all employees, and give team members responsibility for notifying key contacts. Your top clients should usually be notified by executives with all other clients being notified by their account teams.

- The best PR combines giving a prominent news outlet an exclusive on the story and having the CEO write (or have ghost written) a blog post explaining the positives of the deal in more detail.

- The integration team should be assembled prior to the deal close and should initially consist of C-level executives who are already aware of the deal. The goal of the integration team is to solve operational challenges (combining payroll, benefits, etc.) and building cultural bridges between the two teams. Find early wins and opportunities for the two teams to work together.

CHAPTER TEN

SHOULD YOU STAY
OR SHOULD YOU GO?

A good friend of mine sold his agency about 10 years ago. He was near the end of the negotiation, when he ran into a fellow entrepreneur who had sold his business a few years prior. My friend was excited to tell the entrepreneur the good news that he was about to complete an exit. The entrepreneur turned to him and said, "Whatever you do, after you sell your business, don't go cold turkey, it will mess up your life!"

My friend thought the advice was a bit strange—he was expecting a big high five, not a warning! He then went through with the sale and immediately quit the company (cold turkey!), ready to take a much needed break from working.

After a few months of doing nothing, he found that he was fighting with his wife. A lot. Previously, he and his wife had spent some of their time together, but not all of their time. He would be at work for 10 hours a day, and come home happy to spend a few hours every evening with his wife; his wife would spend the day with the kids and friends, and then look forward to time at night with her husband.

Suddenly, with my friend unemployed, the "me" time each of them had was gone. The relationship deteriorated and a short time after selling his company, he and his wife filed for divorce.

SELLING IS HARDER THAN YOU THINK

My friend is not alone. A few years ago, I was on a conference call with entrepreneurs who had sold their companies (one had exited at more than $3 billion!). Everyone shared a similar story—what they imagined would happen post-sale wasn't exactly what transpired. This is not to say that they were unhappy. But in every case, there were unanticipated problems, unexpected sadness, and lots of uncertainty.

WHY SUCCESSFUL EXITS CAN LEAD TO DEPRESSION

For most founders, building an agency is one of their most important, cherished achievements. Those founders are often told by colleagues and advisors that selling their business is the crowning achievement of their business career.

These two goals—building and selling—can be contradictory. The psychiatrist Viktor Frankl notes, "Don't aim at success. The more you aim at it and make it a target, the more you are going to miss it. For success, like happiness, cannot be pursued; it must ensue, and it only does so as the unintended side effect of one's personal dedication to a cause greater than oneself."[1]

---

[1] Viktor Frankl, *Man's Search for Meaning*, (Boston, Mass: Beacon Press, 2006).

When a founder finds purpose through his or her business and then sells the business, this may leave a great void in the founder's psyche, leading to depression and existential angst.

I speak from experience because this happened to me. In 2019, I sold a significant stake in 3Q Digital to outside investors. On paper, this was a career-defining moment for me. An agency that I had started in a coffee shop and grown to more than 300 people was large enough and successful enough to attract professional investors who were ready to lead the company to even greater heights. It was a meaningful financial event for me and a validation of my entrepreneurial abilities.

I assumed that this transaction would simultaneously assuage my ego, reduce my stress, and improve my day-to-day happiness. Instead, I fell into the deepest depression of my life.

It took me many months post-exit to understand and emerge from this rut. And I'm sure with the passing of time, my comprehension will evolve even further. What I can say today, however, is that I've experienced or identified four psychological stressors that can contribute to post-exit depression.

EXIT ANGST, PART ONE: FINDING THE CARROT

Prior to my exit, I was focused on continuous career progression. When I was 25, I was excited to just have a full-time job, even though it barely paid the rent for a rundown apartment in a dodgy part of town. Around 30, I got my first Internet job and became a manager—another goal. At 35, I achieved the title of vice president. At 37, I started my company and spent the next dozen years growing it.

All along the way, there was always a new carrot dangling in front of me: Work hard and I might get to that next level and then seek out an even bigger carrot. And then what may be the biggest carrot of all for an entrepreneur: an exit. As long as I was chasing a carrot, I had purpose. The moment I sold my business, for the first time in my professional life, I had no carrot in front of me.

Entrepreneurs love competition. So, in hindsight, I realized that I really enjoyed being in "the rat race" because, after all, it's a race. Selling my business removed me from the competition that I cherished.

EXIT ANGST, PART TWO: LOSING MEANING

I really felt that my work at 3Q Digital had meaning. Someone once applied Maslow's Hierarchy of Needs to work by noting that you either have a job, a career, or a calling, with a calling being the highest level of self-actualization.[2]

In my case, I always told people that 3Q Digital was on a mission to save clients from inept agencies.

From this perspective, exchanging a business that drives self-actualization for money is a pretty bad deal because, really, what's more important than feeling that you have a calling on earth? And yet, entrepreneurs make this choice all the time.

This is not to say that a founder should never sell his or her business. The decision to sell a business is multifaceted, as discussed in an earlier chapter. That said, for a founder who truly feels that his or her purpose is largely defined by the purpose of that business, selling the business can take a massive psychological toll.

EXIT ANGST, PART THREE: DREAMS VERSUS REALITY

In *Man's Search for Meaning*, Frankl tells the story of a fellow concentration camp inmate who shared a dream with him:

---

[2]A. H. Maslow, A Theory of Human Motivation, *Psychology Review*, 50 (1943), pg. 370-396.

One day a fellow prisoner confided to him that a voice in a strange dream had promised to answer whatever question he wanted to ask. So he asked the voice to tell him when the camp would be liberated. The dream voice replied, March 30th. The man awakened from his dream absolutely thrilled and excited — March 30th was only a few weeks away. Under the torturous conditions in the camp, the man took the dream seriously, believing with all his heart that March 30th would bring salvation. But as the day approached and the news reaching the prisoners remained discouraging, the man took sick.[3]

A day later, the man died. Frankl concludes:

> The ultimate cause of my friend's death was that the expected liberation did not come and he was severely disappointed. This suddenly lowered his body's resistance against the latent typhus infection. The faith in the future and his will to live had become paralyzed and his body fell victim to illness.[4]

Before I sold 3Q Digital, I imagined what it would be like to someday sell my business. In my dream, I saw myself as being exuberantly happy post-sale. First, I thought, I would have enough money to buy a beautiful house, travel to exotic locations, and eat at the finest restaurants, and that this would bring me great joy. Then, I assumed any past challenges around self-worth would magically disappear once the world knew about my exit.

In my mind, all of this would happen instantly after the sale. The reality, of course, could not live up to the dream I had created. The financial freedom was great, but I've since learned about the con-

---

[3]Frankl.
[4]Ibid.

cept of hedonic adaptation.[5] And expecting a business outcome to eliminate self-worth issues is inherently contradictory. It assumes that you'll feel better about yourself through getting the approval of others. The founder lacking self-worth will always point to someone else's bigger and better outcome as an example of why he or she hasn't done enough.

Founders, almost by definition, are dreamers. But when a dream doesn't come true or manifests itself differently than what was imagined, it can be difficult to grapple with reality.

EXIT ANGST, PART FOUR: TOO MANY OPTIONS

A newly exited founder has the freedom to pursue numerous new paths. Start a new business, retire and learn gardening, volunteer at a nonprofit, become a venture capitalist. For many founders, this is the first time in their life with so much optionality. As Sartre says, we are all condemned to freedom.[6] Whatever choice the founder makes implicitly excludes some or all of the other choices.

In a TED talk, Seth Streeter describes nine types of wealth: financial, impact, emotional, social, fun, physical, spiritual, intellectual, and career wealth.[7] In our singular quest for business success, we often ignore some of these crucial types of wealth. There's usually not enough time in the day to do anything but keep the business going and spend some time with the family.

Remove "running a business" from your weekly agenda and you suddenly have 40 (and more likely 80) hours of extra time to allocate. Choosing among all of these equally valuable options can feel overwhelming.

---

[5] Laurie Santos, "The Science of Well-Being," Coursera, Yale University, 2020.
[6] Sartre, Jean-Paul. Existentialism and Human Emotions. Citadel Press, 1957.
[7] Seth Streeter, The Untethered Life: Wealth Redefined, TEDxSantaBarbara, https://www.youtube.com/watch?v=qHNhNjNwGVY.

FIND YOUR SECOND ACT . . . EVENTUALLY

Have you noticed that many great entrepreneurs embark on almost Quixotic quests after leaving their company? Bill Gates has set out to cure the world's diseases. Sergey Brin launched Google X, works on self-driving cars, and developed contact lenses that measure glucose levels. And Tony Hsieh created the Downtown Project in Las Vegas.

I think all of these entrepreneurs discovered they were addicted to purpose. But, as the expression goes, admitting you have a problem is just the first step to recovery. Finding purpose is not easy, and it may be hard to duplicate the serotonin high of that initial purpose-driven business.

At some point, we all retire. For many, this moment comes in their late '60s or early '70s, after having spent 30 or 40 years dedicated to a profession. In popular culture, we talk about retirement as the "Golden Years." It turns out, however, that there's a significant uptick in depression among recently retired people: "The person's sense of self is tied up very strongly in what he or she does for a living; and, with retirement, a sense of loss can occur, leaving a person struggling to understand who they are and what their value is."[8]

I got through my post-sale depression after a few months. In part, I felt better because I realized that there were still plenty of carrots left to harvest at 3Q.

What I'm trying to do instead is to live in the present. As Lao Tzu notes: "If you are depressed you are living in the past. If you are anxious you are living in the future. If you are at peace you are living in the present."[9]

---

[8]How to Deal with Depression After Retirement, VeryWell Mind, January 28, 2021. https://www.verywellmind.com/depression-after-retirement-1067239.
[9]Philosblog, June 19, 2013, https://philosiblog.com/2013/06/19/if-you-are-depressed-you-are-living-in-the-past-if-you-are-anxious-living-in-the-future-if-you-are-at-peace-you-are-living-in-the-moment/.

To be clear, I haven't become the Buddha: I have plenty of worry and anxiety. But I have hope that eventually I'll figure out my next purpose-driven path, and patience that it may take me a while to discover it.

After you sell your agency, realize that you're not alone if you feel a sense of loss at a moment that you may have thought would be nothing but pure joy. Some around you may not understand and may instead deride your pain as a "high class problem." High class problems are still problems!

And give yourself time to find your next act, be it in business or otherwise. Odds are the creativity and drive that helped you build your business will eventually guide you to your next purpose.

WHAT'S NEXT?

Most owners who sell their business are happy with the outcome! The point here is not to dissuade you from selling or to suggest that "Every rose has its thorn," as the '80s hair band Poison wrote.

The point is simply to make you aware that many founders experience some degree of sadness after selling their agency. If you do, you're not alone and you'll likely move beyond it!

Ultimately, you will experience less sadness, anger, confusion, regret—insert your negative adjective here—if you look inward and understand what really drives you to get up every day and run your agency.

Take a moment and create a list of all of your likes and dislikes about running your agency. Here's my list:

LIKES:

- Building businesses
- Helping talented people advance their career
- Helping companies grow
- Being a CEO strokes my vanity
- Feeling relevant and on the bleeding edge of knowledge
- Having a sense of purpose
- Working for myself
- Being busy and working hard

DISLIKES:

- Dealing with HR issues
- Dealing with angry and/or unreasonable clients
- Losing clients/getting fired
- Sacrificing some family time for business obligations
- Sacrificing my health for business obligations

Now look at the deal you're about to sign—does it minimize some or all of your dislikes and maintain or grow your likes? If "having purpose" and "stroking your vanity" are important to you, you can expect to be a little depressed when a few days after you sign your deal, you're demoted from CEO to "advisor" and a new CEO comes in who really doesn't value your opinion.

If you do get depressed after the deal closes, here are a few ideas that might help alleviate the pain:

- **Join a Business Forum Like EO or YPO.** The Entrepreneur's Organization (EO) and the Young Presidents Organization (YPO) are both business networks for founders and C-level executives. To be in EO, you must be the founder of a $1 million or larger business. To be in YPO, you need to be a C-level or founder of a company in excess of $10 million (this amount varies by geography) and join prior to your 45th birthday. In both organizations, you're assigned to a forum—a group of 8 to 12 fellow leaders who meet monthly to discuss their business, personal, and family challenges. The meetings are strictly confidential and follow a methodology that encourages deep sharing.

  Many founders find that it's lonely at the top. A lot of founder problems sound like high-class problems when discussed with someone at a more junior level. EO and YPO resolve that problem—everyone in your forum is your peer and whatever challenge you're facing, there's a good chance that someone in your forum has experienced it in the past and can talk through how they dealt with it. In addition to EO and YPO, The Alliance of Executives and Vistage also offer business forums. You might also consider Tiger21, an organization that only accepts people with at least $20 million of investable assets. This is mainly for investing, but still, it may be comforting to talk to "people like you" if you've had a particularly large exit.

- **The Science of Well-Being**. Dr. Laurie Santos—a professor at Yale University—runs the most popular class on campus, *The Science of Well-Being*, and now offers a video recording of the class for free on Coursera[10] The course starts by asking you to take a happiness assessment online to determine your

---

[10]https://www.coursera.org/learn/the-science-of-well-being.

baseline for happiness. Over several lectures, Dr. Santos discusses the behaviors and actions that scientifically can make people more happy. At the end of the course, you take the happiness assessment again—hopefully your score the second time around will be higher!

- **The Three-Month Rule**. A friend of mine taught me this rule. If he's unhappy at his job, he waits three months and reassesses. If he's still unhappy, he knows it's time to leave. There will be bumps in the road during your post-sale integration. Many of these, however, will be annoying for a few weeks and then will get resolved. If, however, after a few months, you find that the bumps aren't getting smaller and less frequent, and they're bringing you down, it may be time to change course.

STEPPING DOWN FROM CEO OR LEAVING YOUR AGENCY

The first time I sold 3Q, I was dead set on staying in charge of the business—I had energy and a big financial incentive to do so. I felt there was more for me to learn and I was really enjoying my job.

The second time I sold, I was burnt out. It was my third transaction in four years (selling in 2015, buying the company back in 2018, and selling again in 2019). Each of these deals was drawn-out, somewhat contentious, and draining.

I tried to resurrect the energy and excitement I felt after the first deal, but I couldn't make it happen. After a few months, I realized I needed to step down as CEO.

Resigning as CEO takes planning and humility. Here's how I did it after 13 years at the top of my company.

STEP ONE: Fire Yourself from Jobs

I've always believed that the job of an entrepreneur is to fire himself from jobs. In the early days of 3Q (then known as PPC Associates), I was Chief Everything Officer—chief Costco orderer, chief sales pitcher, chief client services head, and so on.

If you're a control freak, this is a great place to be, but if you're trying to build a business beyond yourself, you have to find a way to work *on* the business instead of *in* the business. That means constantly and consciously delegated responsibility for different parts of the business to other team members. By the time I brought in my eventual successor as President, I already had a CFO, CRO, CHRO, head of client service, and head of growth. While I was still involved in a lot of client pitches and client relationships, the business could definitely operate without me.

Indeed, when I took a family trip to Panama for a month and decided to only answer emails once a week, our headquarters did not catch on fire nor did my executive team try to enact a coup d'etat.

To eventually fire yourself completely as CEO, you have to delegate authority for many years, such that when a new CEO takes over, she has a team of leaders surrounding her.

STEP TWO: Create a Trial Run

If possible, your transition out of the CEO role should be gradual. In my case, I initially hired my replacement as a consultant and asked him to give me a comprehensive analysis of my agency's strengths and weaknesses. This was a low-risk scenario for both the agency and the CEO candidate. For 3Q, we could see how the candidate thought and then assess whether his ideas would add value (they did!). The candidate had the opportunity to meet our team and get a taste of 3Q before fully committing.

After the consulting engagement ended, I hired the candidate as president. Initially, he took over responsibility for the operational aspects of the business (finance, HR, operations, client services), while I retained responsibility for sales and marketing. This gave me time to see how he meshed with the team, evaluate his leadership style, and integrate him into the organization.

Historically, 3Q has been an insular organization, promoting from within and regarding outsiders with skepticism. To bring in the candidate as CEO would have been a shock to the system and would have created headwinds for him. By starting him as a consultant and then moving him to president, he was able to gradually move into the organization and be embraced by the team.

STEP THREE: Be a Level Five Leader

In college, I was the editor of the school newspaper. At the end of my tenure, a new editor was elected. I sat down with him as he was starting his reign and asked him about his plans for the year. He was a confident guy and had a ton of radical ideas for the paper. I immediately saw that a lot of these were going to fail and would anger many of the leaders at the newspaper.

So what did I do? Nothing. Instead of explaining why his strategy wasn't going to work, I let him fail. Why? Because I was insecure and I subconsciously thought that if he failed dramatically, it would make my time as editor look fantastic in comparison.

In Jim Collins' book, *Good to Great*, he talks about Level 4 and Level 5 leaders. A Level 4 leader is someone who builds a company by sheer force of will but who doesn't build a next generation of leaders. Thus, after the Level 4 leader departs, the company struggles. A Level 5 leader, however, creates success while running the company but also builds a bench of great leaders who are ready to take his or her place upon retirement.[11]

There are a lot of other things that go into being a Level 5 leader, so I'm not saying that I am the embodiment of this persona, but I can say that when I was at the college newspaper, I was at best a Level 4 leader, because I purposely didn't build strength in my predecessor. I now recognize that the best compliment you can get is not, "You're so much better than the current CEO" but rather, "You found a CEO who took the company to a whole new level." That's what happened with Rob Murray (the consultant I hired who I eventually promoted to CEO), and it's one important aspect of being a Level 5 leader!

STEP FOUR: Respect the Accountability Chart

At 3Q, we've used the Entrepreneur's Operating System (EOS)[12] for many years to manage the business. One of the most important elements in EOS is the weekly Level 10 Meeting (apparently I like concepts that involve levels). In a Level 10 meeting, the executive team sits down and, in 90 minutes, reviews the past week, checks in on quarterly goals, resolves old issues, and discusses new ones.

To make these meetings as effective as possible, it's important that everyone in the meeting is truly a key leader in the business. If there are people who don't actually manage a large part of the business in the Level 10 meeting, they'll either be bored or create distractions.

To determine who gets to join the meeting, you use the accountability chart. This chart outlines who controls the key components of the business. Usually, it means the CEO, potentially a COO/president, head of finance, head of sales, head of marketing, head of HR, head of product/client services, and head of technology.

---

[11]Jim Collins, *Good to Great: Why Some Companies Make the Leap . . . and Others Don't*, (New York: Harper Business, 2001).
[12]https://www.eosworldwide.com/.

If you aren't one of these people, you aren't in the meeting. Period.

Just as you can't be half-pregnant, you can't be half-CEO. Appointing a new CEO while simultaneously continuing to act as CEO is a recipe for failure. Instead, get out of the way, and make it clear to everyone from top executives down that a complete transition has taken place.

STEP FIVE: Blow on the Dandelion

Being a Level Five leader means setting up your replacement for success, and that means providing honest feedback. This feedback, however, comes with two important caveats. First, it should be delivered privately, directly to the new CEO. Publicly airing your differences could sow distrust among the team and, frankly, would be the sort of insecure grandstanding that I want you to avoid.

Second, as soon as you give the feedback, it's up to the new CEO to decide whether it's useful or not. Your role is done. A friend described this as "blowing on the dandelion." You tell someone your opinion, then you blow on the dandelion and watch the seeds disperse into the wind. You no longer think about the issue. You move on. The alternative—continuing to bring up the issue, or talking behind the CEO's back about it—will only create tension, for both you and the new CEO.

ALL THINGS MUST PASS

Change happens.

The A-list movie star of today will be replaced by a new smiling face in a few years. The hot startup getting all the buzz in the trade papers this week may be bankrupt by Fall. The house in which you grew up will eventually be owned by someone else. And, yes, the company you founded will someday need new leadership.

The question is, how will you respond to change? Will you resist it with all of your might? Or, will you embrace it and even enjoy it? With the right strategy and attitude, a great outcome for everyone is not only possible but probable.

SEVEN THINGS TO DO AFTER YOU LEAVE YOUR AGENCY

When most people dream of the ideal retirement, they imagine sitting on a white sand beach under the shade of a towering palm tree, drinking a tropical drink, and watching the waves slowly wash ashore.

This may indeed be your dream—in which case I say, go ahead, make it happen! Assuming that you've sold for enough money that you never need to work again, you've made your dream a reality!

For many founders, however, selling and immediately retiring is not the path they want to take. In her article *What's Next: The Entrepreneur's Epilogue and the Paradox of Success*, Jeanne Odendaal and her team discuss several paths a founder can take after an exit (I've edited the names of each slightly):

1. **The Bon Vivant**. Enjoy life, retire on the beach, or travel the world!

2. **Philanthropy**. Dedicate your time (and money) to a cause you believe in.

3. **Entrepreneurship**. Start a new business.

4. **Invest**. Become a professional investor, either as an angel (individual) or by joining a private equity or venture capital firm (note: early stage venture investing is highly risky and has a high failure rate. Being a successful entrepreneur does not automatically translate into being a successful venture capitalist!).

5. **Teach**. Become a lecturer at a local college or graduate school.

6. **Learn**. Go back to school and get a degree in a subject in which you're interested, or learn guitar and flamenco dancing!

7. **Coach/Advise**. Become a board member or offer advisory services to companies and help them grow.[13]

None of these are mutually exclusive—you can pick several paths and weigh their relative importance accordingly.

KEY TAKEAWAYS FROM THIS CHAPTER

- It's common for entrepreneurs to feel depressed after selling their business. Entrepreneurs may feel that they suddenly lack purpose, are overwhelmed by too much choice, or find that selling simply didn't live up to their high expectations of post-sale bliss.

- Taking time to process your feelings and talking to other entrepreneurs who've gone through the selling process may be helpful. Professional organizations like EO and YPO offer opportunities to connect with post-sale entrepreneurs like yourself.

- The ultimate decision for many entrepreneurs is whether to continue with the company or to leave. Create a pros and cons list for both options to chart your course.

- If you do decide to leave, find and nurture a great successor. Be available as a resource but make sure to give your successor space to create her own vision and get out of her way as soon as you can.

- Post-exit entrepreneurs have many options including teaching, going back to school, becoming a philanthropist, investing, enjoying the good life, or starting a new business.

---

[13] https://yale.app.box.com/s/ye0naovus7anbz875vcrcpzrdskjskgf.

RECOMMENDED READING

- *Second Mountain: How People Move from the Prison of Self to the Joy of Commitment*, by David Brooks

- *Good to Great: Why Some Companies Make the Leap . . . and Others Don't*, by Jim Collins

- *Man's Search for Meaning*, by Viktor Frankl

- *The Psychology of Money: Timeless Lessons on Wealth, Greed, and Happiness*, by Morgan Housel

- *What's Next: The Entrepreneur's Epilogue and the Paradox of Success*, by Jeanne Odendaal, Rick Eigenbrod, A.J.Wasserstein, Mark Agnew, and Brian O'Connor

- *Die with Zero: Getting All You Can from Your Money and Your Life*, by Bill Perkins

- *The Science of Well-Being*, Coursera Online Class by Dr. Laurie Santos

- *Traction: Get a Grip on Your Business*, by Gino Wickman

CHAPTER ELEVEN

REGRETS RIEN
(NO REGRETS)

A few years ago, I went back to Iowa City, Iowa for my 25th high school reunion. I was chatting with a long-lost friend who remarked, "David, it always seemed like you had a plan in life."

This struck me as comical. After all, I'd gone to a college on the East Coast and transferred to a different school after one year, then went to law school and decided not to practice law after I graduated. I then stumbled into a marketing job at a dot com and only started my agency as a short-term solution between entrepreneurial ideas (or so I thought).

When I sold 3Q Digital to Harte Hanks in 2015, I thought that was the end-all, be-all sale. Three years later, I found myself owning 3Q again. When I sold to Erie Street and PSP in 2019, I was excited to partner with my new investors and lead the agency to greater heights. Less than a year later, I voluntarily stepped down from the CEO role and promoted my president to take over.

So yeah, I had plans, but most of those plans never came to fruition!

Selling your agency will likely be a crowning achievement for you—recognition of your prowess at building a great business, as well as a meaningful financial outcome.

At the same time, it won't all go according to plan. You might lose some key employees or important clients, may not be fully aligned with your investors, not get the price you wanted, or have seller's remorse after the deal closes!

Make sure to stop for a moment, look around,
and soak it all in—you've earned it!

My hope is that this book has helped you to avoid, anticipate, or accept bumps, and enabled you to bask in your success rather than dwell on problems.

Most businesses don't grow big enough to be worthy of an acquisition. You built one that did. You created jobs for many people, helped other companies prosper, and executed your vision. Make sure to stop for a moment, look around, and soak it all in—you've earned it!

POSTSCRIPT

LEARNING ON MY DIME

Congrats on getting to the end of the book! When you start the process of selling your agency, the knowledge you gained in this book will help you make informed decisions that ultimately could drive millions of dollars of incremental value while avoiding annoying, costly surprises.

As I noted in the introduction, the majority of agency founders only sell their agency once and are forced to learn the nuances of agency M&A in real-time. This book will help you anticipate and solve challenges before they become deal-killers, and negotiate a deal that protects and promotes your interests.

Reading a book, while a great start, still isn't enough. You wouldn't attempt to fly a jumbo jet after reading a textbook, nor would you offer to perform open-heart surgery on a loved one based on a series of "how to" guides on YouTube.

The sale of your agency will likely be the most important and sizable financial transaction of your life. If there was ever a time in your business career when you needed to pay top dollar for the best experts, this is it.

For this reason, I recommend three experts: an experienced investment banker, an M&A legal team, and . . . me! I haven't spent much time talking about what my M&A advisory firm—Agentic Shift—does, but here's the quick pitch.

Investment bankers and lawyers are vital to a successful M&A outcome, but they have two flaws: first, most of them have never been founders of agencies, so they can't put themselves in your shoes. Second, they have different incentives than you. An investment banker only gets paid the majority of his compensation when you sell, so he wants to your deal done quickly and to the highest bidder. A law firm gets paid on billable hours, so the more complex the contracts and negotiations, the more they get paid.

This is not to say that these experts aren't worthwhile. To the contrary, they're necessary and beneficial. The problem is that there are important aspects of your sale where they're either conflicted, or they simply don't have the right experience to help you succeed.

I learned a lot of tough lessons about selling an agency the hard way—on my own dime! My goal at Agentic Shift is to ensure that you sidestep similar challenges.

My job is to supplement these experts with a founder-centric approach. When you hire Agentic Shift, I act as if I am a co-founder of your agency. I help you decide whether you're ready to sell, interview and negotiate with investment bankers, pick the right law firm, prepare for management presentations, compare and negotiate offers, analyze and edit legal terms, construct a deal communications plan, and figure out your role in your business post-deal.

I learned a lot of tough lessons about selling an agency the hard way—on my own dime! My goal at Agentic Shift is to ensure that you sidestep similar challenges.

For me, this is not about money; selling 3Q has given me the financial security I need. I'm now able to choose how I spend my time and with whom I spend it. This doesn't mean that I'm dirt cheap to hire—I'm not! That said, I am confident that I'll return many times the cost of my services. The ultimate reward for me is to help founders have amazing outcomes. That's the purpose of Agentic Shift. Please reach out to me at AgenticShift.com to start a conversation!

GLOSSARY

Accrual: A method of accounting that records costs and revenue during the month the revenue or expense happened, rather than the month the payment was received or paid.

Acquihire: An acquisition where the main benefit for the buyer is the seller's staff. Acquihires are typically very low value deals, way below a standard multiple for an agency.

Add-on: An add-on acquisition is a type of private equity investment in which a firm acquires a smaller company that is complementary to its existing portfolio. The goal of an add-on acquisition is to grow the firm's portfolio by adding new products, services, or customers.

Adjusted EBITDA: A revised EBITDA figure after removing one-time or unusual costs (such as lawyer fees to prepare for an M&A process). Sellers typically use adjustments to increase their EBITDA in M&A.

Agency of Record: A contract between an agency and a client that establishes the agency as the sole or primary agency for the client.

Asset Sale: An asset sale is a type of transaction in which a company or individual sells one or more specific assets, such as real estate, equipment, patents, or trademarks, rather than selling the entire business or company. In an asset sale, the buyer acquires the assets, but not the liabilities of the seller.

Baseball Arbitration: An arbitration method where both sides must submit a proposal to an arbitrator and the arbitrator must only choose one of the proposals without any modifications. This method tends to force both sides to be more reasonable in their proposals for fear of being too aggressive and having the arbitrator choose the other side's more reasonable proposal.

Board Observer: A person who has a right to attend a board meeting but cannot participate or vote.

Buy-Side: An investment bank representing a buyer looking for companies to acquire.

CAGR: Compound Annual Growth Rate—the average annual growth of a company over a period of years.

CF/DF (Cash-Free, Debt-Free): CF/DF refers to a financial term used in mergers and acquisitions (M&A) to indicate the net value of a company. It's a measure of the enterprise value of a company that excludes cash and cash equivalents, as well as debt obligations.

Closing Costs: Costs associated with an M&A deal that are paid by one or both of the parties, such as lawyers' fees, travel, and investment banker fees.

Common Law: Common law is a legal system that's based on judicial decisions and precedents, rather than on written laws. It's used in many countries, including England, the United States, Canada, and Australia. In common law systems, courts play a central role in interpreting and developing the law, and their decisions set precedents that guide future cases. This means that legal principles and rules are established through the outcome of court cases, rather than through the passage of legislation. Common law systems also rely heavily on legal principles and concepts that have been developed over time through judicial decisions, rather than on a set of written statutes or codes.

Confidential Information Memorandum (CIM): A CIM is a document that's typically used in the process of selling a business or a major asset of a business. It's a comprehensive document that provides detailed information about the company or asset being sold, including financial statements, market analysis, and other information that's relevant to potential buyers. The CIM is usually prepared by the seller, or their advisor, and is provided to prospective buyers under strict confidentiality agreements. The purpose of the CIM is to attract potential buyers and provide them with sufficient information to make an informed decision about whether to pursue an acquisition.

Contingent Payment: A contingent payment is a payment that's dependent on a certain event or condition occurring. It's a payment that's not guaranteed, but rather is conditional on something happening. Contingent payments can be used in a variety of situations, such as in sales contracts, employment agreements, and insurance policies. In the context of mergers and acquisitions, a contingent payment is a type of purchase price structure, where the total amount paid for a business or assets is dependent on certain future events or performance milestones.

Cost of Goods Sold (COGS): Refers to the direct costs associated with producing and selling a product. This includes the cost of materials, labor, and other expenses directly tied to the production of the product, such as factory overhead. COGS does not include indirect expenses such as marketing and administrative costs. The COGS is subtracted from a company's revenue to determine its gross profit.

Cram Down: A cram down in a private company refers to a situation where the owners of a company are forced to accept a restructuring plan or debt repayment plan that they had previously rejected. This can happen when a company is in financial distress and unable to meet its debt obligations, and the creditors or investors propose a plan to restructure the company's debt or equity in order to improve its financial situation.

Data Room: A data room, also known as a virtual data room or VDR, is a secure, online platform that allows users to store and share sensitive documents, such as financial information, legal documents, and other confidential data. Data rooms are primarily used in the context of mergers and acquisitions, where they provide a secure way for potential buyers to access and review confidential information about a company or asset that's being sold.

Drag-Along: A drag-along right, also known as a drag-along provision, is a clause in a shareholder agreement that gives the majority shareholders the ability to force the minority shareholders to sell their shares to a third party. This happens when the majority shareholders have found a buyer who is willing to purchase the entire company, but the minority shareholders are unwilling to sell their shares.

Earnings before Interest, Tax, Deduction, and Amortization (EBITDA): EBITDA is a financial metric that measures a company's operating performance by adjusting its net income for interest, taxes, depreciation, and amortization expenses.

EBITDA is often used as a measure of a company's profitability and cash flow generation ability.

The formula for EBITDA is: **EBITDA = Net Income + Interest + Taxes + Depreciation + Amortization**.

Earnout: An earnout is a type of purchase price structure used in M&A transactions, where a portion of the total purchase price is contingent on the target company achieving certain financial performance milestones or other objectives after the merger or acquisition has been completed.

Employee Stock Option Program (ESOP): An ESOP is a type of retirement plan that allows employees to become owners of the company for which they work by investing in the company's stock. ESOPs are established by companies as a way to provide employees with an ownership stake in the company and to align their interests with those of the company's shareholders.

Exclusivity: Exclusivity in M&A refers to the agreement between a buyer and a seller, in which the seller agrees to not entertain any other offers or engage in any negotiations with other potential buyers for a specified period of time. This period of time is known as the exclusivity period.

Fair Market Value (FMV): FMV is an estimate of the price at which a property or asset would be sold in an open and competitive market. It represents the price that a willing buyer would pay to a willing seller, when both parties have a reasonable knowledge of the relevant facts and neither is under any compulsion to buy or sell.

Family Office: A family office is a private wealth management firm that serves the financial and investment needs of a single family. It provides a wide range of services including financial planning, investment management, tax planning, risk management, accounting, and legal and administrative support. Family offices are typically established by wealthy individuals or families to manage and preserve their wealth over multiple generations.

Fiduciary Duty: A fiduciary duty is a legal obligation to act in the best interest of another party. It's a relationship of trust and confidence between two parties, where one party (the fiduciary) is entrusted to act on behalf of and for the benefit of the other party (the beneficiary).

Flow of Funds: The flow of funds in M&A refers to the movement of money and other financial resources involved in the transaction. This includes the sources of funding for the transaction, such as the buyer's equity and debt financing, as well as the allocation of the purchase price and other transaction costs among the various parties involved.

Generally Accepted Accounting Principles (GAAP): GAAP is a set of guidelines for financial accounting and reporting in the United States. These principles provide a framework for the preparation and presentation of financial statements, such as the balance sheet, income statement, and cash flow statement. They're established by the Financial Accounting Standards Board (FASB) and the American Institute of Certified Public Accountants (AICPA).

Gross Revenue: Gross revenue, also known as gross sales, is the total amount of income generated by a business before any deductions are made. It represents the total amount of money received from the sale of goods or services, and it's typically the first line item on a company's income statement.

Hedonic Adaptation/Hedonic Treadmill: Hedonic adaptation, also known as the "hedonic treadmill" or "hedonic adaptation hypothesis," refers to the tendency for people to quickly adapt to changes in their level of happiness or well-being. This means that, over time, people tend to return to their baseline level of happiness even after experiencing positive or negative events such as getting a promotion, winning the lottery, or going through a divorce. This is also known as trailing twelve months (TTM).

Holding Company (Hold Co): A holding company is a company that owns and manages a portfolio of advertising agencies. These agencies may specialize in different areas of advertising such as digital, television, print, or event marketing, or they may focus on specific industries or geographic regions.

Holding Period: The holding period represents the amount of time a private equity firm owns an acquired business before selling it.

Indication of Intent (IOI): An IOI is a non-binding communication from a potential buyer or seller indicating a desire to enter into a transaction at a certain price or within a certain price range. It's often used in the context of M&A, where a company may send an IOI to another company to express interest in acquiring or merging with them.

Information Rights: Information rights refer to the legal rights of individuals and organizations to access, control, and use information. These rights may include the right to access and obtain information, the right to control the distribution and dissemination of information, and the right to protect the privacy and confidentiality of information.

Last Twelve Months (LTM): LTM typically refers to the period of time covering the most recent 12 months, ending on the most recent month. It's used to represent a company's financial performance over a specific period of time, and is often used to compare the current performance with the performance of the same period in previous years. This is also known as trailing twelve months (TTM).

Lehman Formula: A formula established by the now-defunct investment bank, whereby the investment banker's fee as a percentage of the sales price in an acquisition increases as the sales price increases.

Letter of Intent (LOI): An LOI is a document that outlines the basic terms and conditions of a proposed agreement between two or more parties. It serves as a preliminary document that sets out the key terms and conditions of the proposed agreement and is typically used in business transactions such as mergers, acquisitions, and partnerships.

Leverage: Leverage is the use of borrowed money to amplify an investment's potential return. It involves using a small amount of capital to control a larger amount of assets, such as stocks, bonds, or real estate. By using leverage, an investor can increase the potential return on their investment, but it also increases the potential risk.

Limited Partners: A limited partner is a type of partner in a limited partnership (LP) business structure. In a limited partnership, there are one or more general partners who manage the day-to-day operations of the business and are personally liable for the debts and obligations of the partnership. In contrast, limited partners are not involved in the management of the business and are not personally liable for the debts and obligations of the partnership beyond the amount of their capital contributions.

M&A: Abbreviation for Mergers and Acquisitions.

Management Fee: A private equity management fee is a fee paid by the investors in a private equity fund to the fund's management team for managing the fund's investments. The fee is usually a percentage of the fund's committed capital, typically around 2% per year, and is used to cover the costs of running the fund, such as salaries, office space, and other expenses.

Management Presentation: A management presentation in M&A is a document or set of slides that provide an overview of a company and its operations, financial performance, and strategic goals. It's typically used by the management team of a company that's looking to sell the business, to present to potential buyers, or to investors.

Media Embargo: A media embargo is an agreement between a news organization or journalist and a source of information, that restricts the time or manner in which the information can be published or broadcasted. Embargoes are often used to control the release of sensitive or exclusive information, such as new products, research findings, or government reports.

Multiple Expansion: Multiple expansion occurs when a company acquires another company at a price that has a lower multiple of EBITDA than what the acquiring company is worth, thereby giving the acquiring company an instant return on its investment.

Net Margin: Net margin (also known as net profit margin or net return on sales) is a financial ratio that measures a company's profitability. It represents the percentage of revenue that a company keeps as profit after all expenses have been subtracted. It's calculated by dividing net income (profit) by revenue.

Net Working Capital (NWC): NWC is a measure of a company's liquidity and short-term financial health. It's calculated by subtracting current liabilities from current assets. Current assets are assets that can be converted into cash within one year, such as cash, accounts receivable, and inventory. Current liabilities are debts that must be paid within one year, such as accounts payable, short-term loans, and taxes owed.

No Shop Clause: A no shop clause is a provision in a legal contract, such as a letter of intent, term sheet, or merger agreement, that prohibits one party from soliciting or accepting other offers from third parties while the contract is in effect. This provision is typically included in agreements where one party is looking to acquire or invest in another company, and is intended to prevent the target company from shopping around for a better offer.

Non-Compete Agreement: A non-compete agreement (also known as a non-competition clause or covenant not to compete) is a legal contract in which an employee agrees not to work for a competing company or start their own business that competes with the employer for a certain period of time after leaving the employer's company.

Non-Disclosure Agreement (NDA): An NDA, also known as a confidentiality agreement, is a legal contract between at least two parties in which one or more of the parties agree to not disclose certain confidential information to any third party. This type of agreement is often used to protect sensitive or proprietary business information—such as trade secrets, inventions, financial information, or customer data—from being shared or used without the disclosing party's consent.

Non-Solicitation Agreement: A non-solicitation agreement is a legal agreement between two parties (typically an employer and an employee), in which the employee agrees not to solicit the employer's clients, customers, or other employees for a certain period of time after leaving the company.

Out-Clause: An out-clause, also known as a termination clause or escape clause, is a provision in a contract that allows one or both parties to terminate the contract under certain conditions or circumstances. Out-clauses are typically included in contracts to provide a way for a party to end the contract early, without penalty or liability, should certain events occur or if certain conditions are not met.

Par Value: Par value, also known as face value or nominal value, is the value assigned to a security, typically a stock, by the issuing company. The par value is usually a very small amount, such as $0.01 or $1.00 per share, and is used primarily for accounting and legal purposes. It has no relation to the market value of the stock, which is determined by supply and demand in the market.

Pari-Passu: Pari-passu is a Latin phrase meaning "on equal footing" or "with equal rights." In the context of finance and investments, it's used to describe a situation where multiple creditors or investors have equal rights and priority in receiving payments or distributions of assets. This means that each creditor or investor is entitled to receive a pro rata share of the payments or assets based on the amount they're owed or invested.

Payment in Kind (PIK): PIK refers to a type of financing in which a borrower is not required to make cash payments of interest or principal, but instead makes payments in the form of additional debt or equity. In other words, instead of paying cash, the borrower agrees to pay interest by issuing new debt or equity securities to the lender. This type of financing is typically used by companies that have difficulty generating cash flow to meet debt payments.

Platform: In private equity, a platform refers to a company that serves as the foundation or base for a series of acquisitions in a specific industry or market. The private equity firm acquires the platform company first, and then uses it as a vehicle to make additional acquisitions in the same industry, creating a larger and more diversified company. This is called a roll-up strategy.

Preferred Stock: Preferred stock is a type of corporate equity that has characteristics of both common stock and debt. Preferred stockholders have a higher claim on the assets and earnings of a company than common stockholders, but a lower claim than bondholders. Preferred stock typically pays a fixed dividend, similar to a bond coupon, and has a higher priority in the event of a liquidation or bankruptcy.

Preferred Return: Preferred return refers to the minimum return that investors in a private equity or real estate fund expect to receive before the general partners or fund managers start to receive carried interest. It's usually a fixed percentage of the total capital invested, such as 8% or 10%. The preferred return is paid out of the fund's cash flow or from the sale of assets and is typically paid out before the fund's profits are distributed to the general partners or fund managers.

Private Equity: Private equity refers to a type of investment in which investors (typically large institutional investors, such as pension funds, endowments, and high-net-worth individuals) provide capital to privately held companies in exchange for an ownership stake. Private equity investors typically target companies that have the potential for significant growth or that are undervalued and in need of operational improvements.

Pro Rata: Pro rata refers to the allocation of something in proportion to a known quantity. In finance, the term is often used to refer to the proportionate allocation of something, such as shares of stock, investment capital, or rights, among a group of investors or stakeholders.

Qualified Small Business Stock (QSBS): QSBS refers to stocks of a qualified small business corporation that meet certain requirements under the United States Internal Revenue Code. If an individual holds QSBS for more than five years, the gain on the sale of the stock is taxed at a lower capital gains rate (0% to 20%) than the individual's regular tax rate. This tax incentive is intended to encourage investment in small businesses.

Quality of Earnings Report (QofE): Quality of earnings refers to the level of transparency, consistency, and reliability of a company's reported financial results. It's an analysis of the underlying financial and operational factors that determine a company's reported earnings, and assesses the sustainability of those earnings.

Recapitalization (Recap): Recapitalization is a financial restructuring that changes the capital structure of a company. It can involve a variety of actions such as issuing new shares of stock, selling or issuing debt, or buying back shares of stock. The goal of a recapitalization is to improve the financial health of the company and increase the value of the company for shareholders.

Retrade: Retrade, also known as "backtracking," refers to the process of renegotiating the terms of a previously agreed upon business deal, typically after the deal has been signed, but before it has been closed or implemented. This can happen for a variety of reasons, such as new information coming to light or a change in market conditions. Retrading can cause delays and uncertainty in the completion of a deal, and can also lead to the breakdown of the deal if the parties are unable to come to new terms.

Right to Repurchase: A right to repurchase, also known as a "right of first refusal" or "ROFR," is a contractual agreement that gives the holder of the right the option to purchase a specific asset or property before it's offered to other potential buyers. This type of agreement is often used to protect a current owner's interests in the asset, such as in the case of a business partnership dissolution, or to ensure that a specific buyer is given the opportunity to purchase an asset before it's sold to a third party. The right to repurchase may be triggered by specific events, such as the sale of the asset, or it may be a standing agreement that's always in effect.

Roll or Rollover: A stock rollover is a type of transaction in which an investor exchanges shares of one company's stock for shares of another company's stock, without selling the original shares and recognizing a capital gain or loss. This type of transaction is commonly used in mergers and acquisitions, where shareholders of the acquired company exchange their shares for shares of the acquiring company. The rollover allows the investor to maintain their investment in the same industry or sector, while avoiding any immediate tax consequences. However, it's important to note that the investor may still be subject to taxes on the new shares when they're sold or when the shares are converted to cash.

Roll-Up: A private equity roll-up, also known as a platform acquisition, is a strategy used by private equity firms to build a larger company by acquiring and consolidating multiple smaller companies in the same industry. This strategy is used to achieve economies of scale and create a more competitive company through cost savings and increased market share.

Secured Debt: Secured debt refers to a type of debt that's backed by collateral, such as property, equipment, or inventory. The collateral serves as security for the lender, ensuring they have a way to recoup their investment in the event of default by the borrower. Secured debt is generally considered to be less risky for the lender than unsecured debt, as they have a tangible asset that they can seize and sell to recover the value of the loan. Examples of secured debt include mortgages, car loans, and equipment loans. In the event of default, the lender can foreclose on the property, repossess the car or equipment, and sell it to repay the loan.

Security Purchase Agreement (SPA): A security purchase agreement (SPA) is a legal contract that outlines the terms and conditions of a transaction in which one party, the purchaser, agrees to buy securities, such as stocks, bonds, or options, from another party, the seller. The SPA typically includes information, such as the type and number of securities to be purchased, the purchase price, any contingencies or conditions that must be met before the purchase can be completed, and the rights and obligations of the parties involved. It also outlines representations and warranties made by the seller, such as the accuracy of financial statements and the legality of the securities being sold. Additionally, it may include restrictive covenants, such as lock-up agreements, and termination rights for both parties. The SPA is a legally binding document that's typically negotiated and executed by the parties' legal counsels before the transaction can close.

Sell-Side: The sell-side refers to the aspect of the financial markets where securities are sold by issuers, investment banks, and other financial institutions to investors, such as institutional investors and retail investors. The sell-side includes such activities as underwriting new securities, creating and distributing research, and providing advice on mergers and acquisitions. It's in contrast to the buy-side, which refers to the aspect of the financial markets where securities are purchased by investors, such as hedge funds, mutual funds, and pension funds. The buy-side typically relies on the research and advice provided by the sell-side.

Stock Sale: In a stock sale, a company sells ownership shares in the company to a buyer. This type of transaction results in the buyer becoming a shareholder in the company and gaining a percentage of ownership in the company. A stock sale does not involve the transfer of specific assets of the company, but rather the transfer of ownership in the company as a whole.

Stock Vesting: Stock vesting refers to the process by which an employee earns the right to own a certain number of shares of stock in a company over a specified period of time. The shares are typically awarded as part of a compensation package, such as a signing bonus or long-term incentive plan.

Stock Vesting Acceleration: Stock acceleration is a provision in a stock option plan that allows for the accelerated vesting of stock options in certain situations, such as the termination of an employee's employment or a change in control of the company. This means that the employee will be able to exercise their stock options and receive the shares earlier than they would have under the normal vesting schedule.

Strategics: A strategic acquirer in M&A is a company that makes an acquisition in order to achieve a specific strategic goal or gain a specific benefit. These acquisitions are typically made to gain access to new markets, customers, products, technologies, or other resources that will help the acquiring company to grow or improve its operations.

Success Fee: A success fee is a fee charged by a professional advisor, such as an investment bank, a consultant, or a lawyer, to a client for achieving a specific objective or reaching a certain performance level. This fee is typically a percentage of the total transaction value or the amount of money saved by the client as a result of the advisor's work. Success fees are often used in investment banking, where they're charged to clients for completing a successful merger, acquisition, or other financial transaction, but also used in other professional services such as consulting and legal representation, where the outcome of the services is tied to a specific outcome.

Tag-Along Rights: Tag-along rights, also known as "co-sale rights," are rights given to minority shareholders in a company that allow them to join in the sale of the company's shares when a majority shareholder or group of shareholders decides to sell their shares. These rights give minority shareholders the option to sell their shares alongside the majority shareholders at the same price and on the same terms. The purpose of tag-along rights is to protect the interests of minority shareholders and prevent them from being left behind in the event of a sale of the company's shares. They can also be used as a tool to avoid a situation where majority shareholders could sell their shares to a third party without the consent of the minority shareholders.

Tail: A tail clause in an investment banking contract is a provision that specifies a period of time after the completion of a transaction or the termination of a contract during which certain terms and conditions will continue to apply. It's also known as "survival clause" or "endurance clause." This period of time is referred to as the "tail" of the contract.

Teaser: An investment banking teaser, also known as a "teaser memo" or "teaser pitch," is a short, preliminary document that's used by investment banks to provide a high-level overview of a potential transaction or investment opportunity to potential clients or investors. The teaser typically includes information about the company or asset being offered, its financial performance and projections, and the reasons why the investment bank believes it's a good opportunity.

Waterfall: A financial waterfall, also known as a "cash flow waterfall," is a method of allocating cash flow or returns from an investment among different parties in a structured way. This is typically used in private equity and real estate investments, where multiple investors have put money into a fund or project, and the returns need to be distributed among them in a predetermined manner.

ACKNOWLEDGEMENTS

Thank you to Robert Glazer for putting in many hours reviewing and often correcting this book. You added so many amazing points and really took the book from "good to great" (I hope!).

Much of my knowledge about the M&A space came from the top-notch investment bankers I worked with—David Clark, who got us an outstanding deal in 2015, and Sanjay Chadda, who guided us through an extra-long negotiation in 2019, and then an extra-extra-long negotiation in 2022. Thank you also to Ron Wagner at Garros Group, who gave me great feedback on the initial drafts of this book.

None of the deals discussed in this book would have been possible without the leaders at 3Q that worked tirelessly to make them happen: Dave Yoo, Will Lin, Maury Domengeaux, Scott Rayden, and Brian Grabowski (2014, 2015); Maury Domengeaux, Steve Schlossareck, Scott Rayden, Diego Rovira, and Brian Grabowski (2018, 2019); and Rob Murray and Shane Kern (2021). What I appreciate most about doing these deals with you is the integrity, drive, and team spirit you exhibited throughout every step of the process.

You can't sell an agency if there isn't a buyer! Thank you to Robert Philpott at Harte Hanks for seeing the potential of 3Q and partnering with us to make our first transaction happen. Thanks also to Penny Pritzker, Troy Noard, and Peter Berghoff at PSP Partners, and to Terry Graunke and Jerry Graunke at Erie Street Growth Partners for joining forces to invest in and scale 3Q in 2019. And thank you to Dimi Albers and the team at DEPT for integrating us into the rocket ship that is DEPT in 2022.

As I'm not the most detail-oriented person in the world, this book would not have been possible without the great editorial, creative, and publishing oversight of Linda Popky and her team.

And, of course, to the more than a thousand talented 3Qers with whom I worked from 2008-2023, none of this would have been possible without your relentless drive to "act like it's your money" and "save clients from inept agencies." While I'm proud of selling 3Q three times, the most fulfilling aspect of creating 3Q has always been mentoring you and watching you become world-renown leaders in your own right. I hope that you will continue to pay it forward—whether at 3Q, your own agency, or through another company.

ABOUT THE AUTHORS/
AGENTIC SHIFT

DAVID RODNITZKY

David Rodnitzky is the founder of Agentic Shift, a consulting firm that advises marketing agency founders who are considering or actively conducting a sale of their agency business.

David's marketing career began in 2000, when he accepted a job at Rentals.com, an online property management startup. At Rentals.com, David reallocated $50,000 a month of PR and branding spend to the nascent field of search engine marketing (SEM), building partnerships with GoTo.net (later Yahoo Search Marketing) and Google, and driving thousands of new visitors for pennies a click.

In 2001, David joined FindLaw, the largest online legal site in the world. David continued his work in search engine marketing, negotiating a multi-year search advertising deal with MSN (including guaranteed third placement on the word "lawyer" for $.25 a click!). During David's tenure, FindLaw's online traffic grew to be one of the top 300 websites in the United States. In 2004, he was invited by Sheryl Sandberg to present to the entire Google advertising team on best practices in Google advertising.

In 2004, David joined Adteractive, an online lead generation company. David increased the company's online marketing spend from

$100,000 a month to over $1.5 million a month, developed an algorithm for SEM bid management, and invented several SEM strategies that became best practices in the industry, including the "Golden Corral" keyword management process.

David joined Mercantila.com, an ecommerce drop shipper in 2007 as Vice President of Advertising. At Mercantila, David managed a 15-person team on two continents and built the first profitable marketing campaigns in the company's history.

In 2008, David launched PPCAdBuying.com, later known as PPC Associates and, eventually, 3Q Digital. David started the agency in a coffee shop in Pacifica, California. Over a 13-year period running 3Q Digital, David's accomplishments include:

- Scaling the business to over 300 employees and more than $60 million annual revenue.

- Increasing advertising spend under management to over $1.5 billion annually.

- Expanding the company offerings from SEM management to full-service performance marketing.

- Opening offices in over a dozen cities on three continents.

- Co-creating the Alpha Beta Account Structure and Lin-Rodnitzky Ratio methodologies that are widely used in the SEM industry.

- Being recognized as Google's largest agency partner.

- Being regularly quoted by the *Wall Street Journal, The New York Times, Washington Post, Newsweek, Entrepreneur Magazine*, and numerous other publications.

- Being awarded the University of Iowa's 2021 Alumni Entrepreneur of the Year.

David sold 3Q to Harte Hanks in 2015, led a management buyout of the business in 2018, sold it to Erie Street Growth Partners and PSP Partners in 2018, and worked with his PE sponsors to sell 3Q to DEPT (a Carlyle Group Company) in 2022.

In 2023, David launched Agentic Shift. Agentic Shift leverages David's multiple M&A experiences to help agency founders learn on someone else's dime, as they consider and execute a sale of their agency.

David lives in San Mateo, CA with his wife, two sons, and their dog.

ROBERT GLAZER

Robert Glazer is the founder and chairman of the board of global partner marketing agency Acceleration Partners. A serial entrepreneur, award-winning executive, bestselling author, and keynote speaker, Bob has a passion for helping individuals and organizations build their capacity and elevate their performance.

Outside of work, Bob can likely be found skiing, cycling, reading, traveling, spending quality time with his family, or overseeing some sort of home renovation project.